D1055611

Her Ladyship's

GUIDE TO
RUNNING ONE'S HOME

Her Ladyship's
GUIDE TO
RUNNING ONE'S HOME

CAROLINE TAGGART

National Trust

*For Cec, without whose wisdom – and boundless
enthusiasm for cleaning – this book would have
been very much shorter than it is.*

First published in the United Kingdom in 2012 by
National Trust Books
10 Southcombe Street
London
W14 0RA

An imprint of Anova Books Company Ltd

ISBN 978 19078 9213 4

A CIP catalogue record for this book is available from the British Library.

21 20 19 18 17 16 15 14 13 12
10 9 8 7 6 5 4 3 2 1

Reproduction by Mission Productions, Hong Kong
Printed and bound by Toppan Leefung Printing Ltd, China

This book can be ordered direct from the publisher at the website
www.anovabooks.com, or try your local bookshop. Also available at
National Trust shops and www.nationaltrustbooks.co.uk.

**Publisher's note: The advice in this book is intended for
general domestic use and is no substitute for specialist care of
antiques and other valuable furniture and fittings.**

Contents

ACKNOWLEDGEMENTS

Many thanks to Niki, Rebecca and Ros, who all run their homes more efficiently than I do and who made substantial contributions to this book; and to everyone who features as 'a friend of Her Ladyship': Ann for making the best salads, Chris for pointing out the dangers of email, Dom for coming early to my parties, Gavin, Cristina and Bruce for being good dog owners and a great dog, Liz for her insight into the folding of towels, Lorraine for giving excellent cocktail parties and Rosey for being the sort of mother most children would kill to have.

Thanks also to Cathy, Nicola and everyone at Batsford and the National Trust for making the book happen.

INTRODUCTION

In the nineteenth century Mrs Beeton was inspired to embark on
her famous *Book of Household Management* because, married at the
age of 20, she found herself in charge of a household that
included a cook, a gardener, a kitchen maid and a housemaid and
had no idea how to supervise them. Subsequent generations,
learning to cope with fewer servants, were better instructed, both
at their mother's knee and at school. In 1906 the domestic science
house at Cheltenham Ladies' College offered courses in 'practical
and high-class cooking, dressmaking, laundry and housewifery'.
In the 1940s, 'housework' was still part of the curriculum in many
state schools, whose pupils would grow up to have no servants at
all. But these courses are largely a thing of the past and the late
twentieth-century mother seems to have been sadly lacking in
knees at which her daughters could learn domestic skills.

Mrs Beeton's modern equivalent, whether married or single,
probably does her own cooking and most of her own housework.
Even so, she wants to run her house 'properly' – perhaps without
having a clear idea of what 'properly' means. She wants to live in
pleasant surroundings without being a slave to housework. She
wants to entertain her friends and invite people to stay without
committing social *faux pas*. Her 'staff' is likely to be limited to a
cleaner who comes in for a couple of hours twice a week and an

au pair or nanny if she has small children, but these people still need to be recruited and supervised. She doesn't have a butler to serve wine at dinner parties, nor a housekeeper to make sure the linen is in good order. She needs all the skills that her great-great-grandmother took for granted – and she needs to juggle them with the demands of going to work.

These are the predicaments with which this book aims to deal – and where Her Ladyship comes in.

When it comes to housework, Her Ladyship relies on two age-old maxims and one rather newer one: *The house is not a monster, nor is it your master.* 'Prevention is better than cure', 'A stitch in time saves nine' and, although she would not normally demean herself to use the expression, 'Don't sweat the small stuff'. The house is not a monster, nor is it your master. Gone are the days when, if you didn't keep your house clean, you could be dragged before a 'court of nuisance' and given the medieval equivalent of an ASBO. Dealing with the modern home requires a modicum of practical knowledge, a systematic approach and a few straightforward hints and short cuts: the aim is to keep your home looking as it should do, without reducing you to a state of nervous collapse.

Much the same applies to giving dinner parties or inviting friends for the weekend. Ninety per cent of it comes down to careful planning and an understanding that your guests are on your side – they *want* to have a good time. Hiring staff? Common sense, attention to detail and basic courtesy will take you a very long way.

At the beginning of her first chapter, Mrs Beeton quoted from the Biblical book of Proverbs. The Bible is talking about a virtuous woman; Mrs Beeton obviously took this to mean the successful mistress of a household:

> *Strength, and honour are her clothing; and she shall rejoice in time to come. She openeth her mouth with wisdom; and in her tongue is the law of kindness. She looketh well to the ways of her household; and eateth not the bread of idleness. Her children arise up, and call her blessed; her husband also, and he praiseth her.*

In this day and age, to expect your children to rise up and call you blessed is perhaps to court disappointment. On the other hand, dear Reader, Her Ladyship suggests – gently – that if you follow her advice on matters domestic, you may find room, if not for the bread of idleness, at least for the occasional chocolate of relaxation.

Author's note: much of this book makes the same assumption that Mrs Beeton did: that her readership was entirely female. For Her Ladyship this is, however, a matter of authorial convenience. She has no wish to offend anyone and would be very interested to hear from any of her male readers who know how to change the dustbag on the vacuum cleaner or would think of putting flowers in a guest bedroom.

One

HOUSEKEEPING
DAY BY DAY

*All work is coloured by the spectacles worn. Look on it as fearful
drudgery and it will never be anything else. See it as a job
supremely worth doing, some of it creative, some more humdrum,
but all demanding one's best, then running the home without help
becomes a challenge and rewarding in itself.*

Kay Smallshaw, *How to Run Your Home without Help,* 1949

As late as the 1950s homemaking experts were laying down
frightening rules about the amount of housework a woman – and
it was always a woman – needed to do every day.

A women's magazine of the period described one married
woman's routine as running a carpet sweeper through her house,
dusting the bedroom and sitting room and wiping round the
bathroom basin every morning before going to work. The same
woman also tried to do some 'special cleaning' in the evenings:
vacuuming the carpet one evening, polishing the furniture the
next. Washing and ironing were usually 'fitted in' at the weekends.
'In this way,' the magazine summarised approvingly, 'she has a
pleasantly kept house and yet is free to spend most evenings as she
and her husband wish.' (After she has prepared a meal, that is,
and done that day's 'special cleaning'.)

Her Ladyship, were the word to be in her vocabulary, would
say, 'Puh-leeese!' The only house that needs to be treated as

carefully as this is one that is open to the public. She also ventures to suggest that the advent of children would run rings round this happy domestic routine. Her Ladyship's first (and perhaps only) rule of housekeeping is 'Do not become a slave to the house'. The house is not the enemy. It needs to be clean – or reasonably clean; it doesn't need to look as if it belongs in the pages of *House Beautiful* and it will be more comfortable to live in if it doesn't. A little bit of dust and the odd cushion out of place never hurt anyone. A wise friend of Her Ladyship's, the mother of two sons now in their twenties, puts it this way: 'My boys aren't going to remember me because I let them grow up in a really clean house. They're going to remember that I took them camping, cooked good food and made their friends feel at home.'

That said, housework still needs to be done. Today's technology makes it unnecessary (and today's lifestyle makes it impossible) to devote a whole day to washing, as our grandmothers did every Monday. Most people find it more convenient to do a load of washing whenever there is enough of the same thing – whether it be cottons, coloureds or delicates – to make it worthwhile.

It may, however, help to have a timetable for other tasks: always do the ironing on Tuesday, vacuuming on Wednesday, etc. The problem here is that an invitation to go out on a Tuesday night throws the system into disarray. You may prefer to do all your routine housework on a Saturday, though this system too has its drawbacks when you go away for the weekend.

Perhaps the most sensible piece of advice is to find a system that suits your lifestyle and to adhere to it as far as is possible without it becoming a millstone around your neck. A bathroom that is routinely cleaned on a Thursday can be cleaned on a Friday without the world coming to an end; ironing that is usually done at the weekend can be left unironed for a few days if a more alluring invitation comes along.

One piece of routine that *is* worth sticking to, however, is a very quick tidy up before you go to bed. This is merely so that your living room doesn't look as if a bomb has hit it the next morning. Plump up cushions, put magazines into the rack (or into a neat pile, even if it is a pile of one – don't leave them lying open on the sofa), put the TV and game console remotes back where they belong. Put glasses, coffee cups or plates from a late-night snack in the dishwasher, or at least stack them beside the sink – see the notes about clearing up after dinner parties on page 112.

Even if you can be bothered to do none of these things, please, if anyone in the household smokes, make the effort to empty ashtrays, rather than leaving them to pollute the atmosphere still further. Don't empty them straight into the bin: pour the contents on to a sheet of newspaper or into a plastic bag, wrap or seal them and put the sealed package into the bin. And by 'bin', Her Ladyship means a lidded bin in the kitchen, rather than an open wastepaper basket in the living room.

If you have someone to help with the cleaning, it is worth being particularly disciplined about tidying up the day before she comes. You are paying her to vacuum under the bed and scrub the shower cubicle, not put your newspapers in the recycling bin. If you leave your home in a mess, the cleaner may have to spend half an hour of her allotted two hours clearing up before she can start her real work – and she may throw away things you want to keep, or put them away in the wrong place. Ten minutes of your time making sure this doesn't happen will be ten minutes well spent.

Some tips about storage

Tidiness is not the same as cleanliness, but it goes a long way towards creating a good first impression when you or anyone else walk into a room. Putting things away is the easiest way to make the home look neat. It is impossible to have too much storage space, so be alert to opportunities.

• Make use of often overlooked spaces, such as nooks and crannies under the stairs or in corners.

• Have hooks inside the wardrobe door on which to hang ties, belts and scarves. Use the inside of doors in other rooms, too: put up a spice rack in the kitchen or a container for cosmetics in the bathroom.

• Build bookshelves and kitchen cabinets to the ceiling and store rarely used items at the top. Make sure you possess a stepladder high enough to reach the top shelves when necessary.

• If existing shelves and cabinets do not reach the ceiling, use the top of them as a shelf and, again, store 'once in a blue moon' items there. They will probably need to be washed before they can be used but, given the infrequency with which blue moons occur, this should not be too much of a hardship.

More tips about storage

• Make use of under-cabinet space in the kitchen or dining room too: install a shelf deep enough to hold a selection of glasses or mugs, or a slotted rack in which plates can be stacked vertically.

• Don't forget overhead space: hang pots and pans from a rack on the kitchen ceiling. Do this only if it is high enough, however: you don't want to have to duck every time you turn round to pick up the pepper mill.

• Use stacking baskets (wire or wicker) or colourful plastic tubs one on top of the other to maximise storage space in wardrobes, in home offices, under tables and in corners.

• When buying new beds or coffee tables, buy the kind that has drawers underneath. This not only provides extra storage space, it reduces the number of awkward places you have to vacuum or sweep.

• Make storage items attractive: invest in an old trunk of the kind seen in Agatha Christie adaptations and keep spare blankets in it; use handsome wicker baskets for DVDs.

You've got mail

It is a sad fact of modern life that most of the 'snail mail' anyone receives is junk, so it can be hard to work up the enthusiasm to deal with it. The implications of not opening and therefore not paying the electricity bill are beyond the scope of this book, but an accumulation of post does constitute unnecessary clutter. If you are prone to allowing days or weeks to pass before you open anything except a birthday card, Her Ladyship advocates these measures:

• The moment you pick up the post, identify the pieces that can go straight into the recycling and throw them away at once. Catalogues from which you are never going to buy anything and offers of interest-free periods if you take on a new credit card do not need even to be opened. Nor does anything addressed to 'the occupier' unless you have moved home in the last three months.
• Put post that you do need to deal with – bills, magazines that you want to read, personal letters that require an answer – into a neat heap and always keep it in the same place. This could be a table in the hall, a particular position on your desk or anywhere else where it can be out of the way but not completely overlooked.
• Add 'dealing with post' to your weekly schedule and do it.
• Minimise junk by removing yourself from lists and accepting any offer to go 'paper free'. There is no concrete evidence that putting up a sign saying 'No junk mail' has any effect whatsoever, though in theory subscribing to a mail preference service does.

How often?

To keep the home at a reasonable level of cleanliness, routine tasks should be carried out at least once a week. These tasks include dusting, vacuuming or sweeping floors, cleaning the bathroom(s) and cleaning the work surfaces and hob in the kitchen. If you have a household full of dogs or children with muddy feet and sticky fingers, this may have to increase to every day – or even more. An element of common sense must be invoked here. Look around you. Is your home dirtier than you would like it to be? Then it is time to clean it.

It is foolish to attempt to lay down hard and fast rules for the frequency of 'every so often' tasks. If you cook a weekly roast you will probably find it desirable to clean the oven once a month (though roasting bags are a great saver of mess here); if not, you may find that once every six months is enough. The only rule that should be obeyed in a 'hard and fast' manner is that spillages should be cleaned up immediately: meat juices that drip on to the bottom of the oven can be wiped away without difficulty; they become a considerable chore if allowed to harden or (heaven forfend) are left untackled when the oven is used again.

A useful guideline for 'once in a blue moon' tasks: clean things before they become horribly dirty and *learn to recognise when that is likely to be*. If it helps, keep a 'housekeeping diary'. If the oven or the kitchen blinds or the living room curtains were disgusting last time you cleaned them after an interval of x months, make a note to clean them after y months, where y is a number smaller than x.

One other common-sense tip: if cleaning a house with more than one storey, start at the top and work down. Any dust raised by cleaning the upstairs will, self-evidently, fall downwards, which is annoying if the downstairs has just been cleaned. Kay Smallshaw, writing in the 1940s for stay-at-home wives doing all their own housework,

If cleaning a house with more than one storey, start at the top and work down.

recommended that the downstairs be made 'presentable' first, 'with priority given to the front of the house, where, if visitors were to call, they could be received'. Pshaw, says Her Ladyship. Now that the formal 'morning call' is no longer a feature of most people's social calendar, the laws of gravity take precedence. Visitors who call on the off chance should be happy to sit at the kitchen table with a mug of coffee: if necessary, you can simply ask them to excuse the mess. The uninvited, frankly, must take you as they find you, however welcome they may be.

Vacuuming and sweeping

The maxim that prevention is better than cure holds true in housekeeping as it does elsewhere. A doormat just outside or inside each external door encourages visitors and residents alike to wipe their feet before entering. Outside has the advantage that visitors, having rung the bell, have a moment or two to notice the presence of a mat and to make use of it. Coconut matting is best, and can be turned over and beaten with a broom handle every so often to prevent it becoming clogged with dirt and dust. 'Every so often' might mean every two days if your household has a lot of foot traffic, once a week or even once a fortnight if you are on your own. Plain coconut matting doesn't have a 'wrong' side, so once you have turned it over you can leave it that way up until the next time.

If you live somewhere where outdoor shoes are routinely going to be covered in mud (or worse), get into the habit of changing into clean indoor shoes as soon as you come in.

Bearing in mind that much of what we call 'dust' is actually made up of flakes of skin and other human detritus, Her Ladyship has heard a story (surely apocryphal?) of a woman who, in a desperate attempt to keep her home clean, threatened to vacuum her husband all over the moment he came in the door each evening. Perhaps the housewife's truest friend is a loofah, strategically placed to encourage all members of the household to exfoliate thoroughly in the shower.

However, no amount of shoe-changing or exfoliation can circumvent the fact that carpets do need to be vacuumed or swept. Not only does it keep them clean, it prevents the build-up of house-dust mites (to which many people are allergic) and other pests and protects the fibres, making the carpet last longer. So vacuuming is genuinely a money-saving activity. Her Ladyship advocates doing 'the bits that show' at least once a week and moving the furniture into the middle of the room and vacuuming behind it once a month. You never know when a telephone engineer is going to need to gain access to the socket behind the sofa, so – to avoid the embarrassment of showering him with layers of dust – this task cannot be neglected ad infinitum.

Her Ladyship advocates doing 'the bits that show' at least once a week.

Vacuum cleaners come with a number of attachments that should be exploited to the full: the upholstery attachment can be run up and down the curtains, avoiding the need for frequent dry-cleaning. Turn the suction level down to low when you do this to stop the machine swallowing the material. Other attachments make it easy to reach awkward corners, to remove dust from the skirting board and to clean that gap between the cushions on the sofa which mysteriously attracts so much debris.

If your vacuum cleaner has a bag, change it before it is full. Empty a bagless one after every two or three uses (more if quantities of dog hair are involved) and clean the filters, following the manufacturer's instructions, to keep the machine operating efficiently. Experience will show how often this needs to be done.

With rugs, beating is preferable to vacuuming. Take the rug outside, hang it wrong side out over the washing line, the balcony wall or the back of a sturdy chair and beat it until the dust ceases to fly. Smaller rugs can simply be shaken, which provides a vigorous upper-body workout for those who care about such things.

Beating can be done with a broom handle, but there has lately been a revival in the Victorian-style carpet beater (sometimes – pretentiously, in Her Ladyship's view – known by its Dutch name of *mattenklopper*). This handy device was a feature of every household's cleaning equipment before vacuum cleaners became generally affordable in the early twentieth century. Made of wicker or cane, the modern version looks rather like a badminton racket on which the strings have been woven into Celtic knots, but is nevertheless an effective tool.

If by any chance you own the sort of room in which the carpet is removed and rolled up to provide a dance floor for parties (see page 124), vacuum the carpet as you roll it: the act of rolling opens up the structure of a pile carpet, releasing ingrained dirt which can then be hoovered up. Take the opportunity to vacuum both sides of the underlay too.

The advice given here may not be suitable for a Persian or other luxurious rug that you and your insurance company treasure. If that is what you possess, lay it over a rigid board covered with acid-free paper, and vacuum the area it supports with the small, flat head of the vacuum cleaner. When you have finished, move the board and progress to the next section.

Cleaning floors

Wooden floors should be swept as often as every day if there is a lot of traffic, and certainly once a week. In the kitchen they also need to be mopped to clear up spillages. Polishing wooden floors makes them slippery, so should be done infrequently and when any unsteady or clumsy members of

Wooden floors should be swept as often as every day if there is a lot of traffic, and certainly once a week.

the household are away for a few days. Tucking a duster smeared with beeswax round a swivel-headed mop is a quick and easy way of performing this task; for large areas, it is worth hiring an electric polisher once a year to do the job properly.

Hardwood floors are particularly vulnerable to scratching. Keep pets' nails trimmed and lift furniture rather than drag it (all too easy to forget when drawing a chair closer to the dining table). See page 124 for advice on protecting floors when you give a party.

Sweep or vacuum cork and linoleum floors regularly. Cork should not be mopped or washed; instead, clean and wax it with products designed for the purpose. Linoleum may be washed with warm water and washing-up liquid, but use as little water and as little washing-up liquid as possible – it ought not to be soaked. Mrs Beeton recommended rubbing milk over clean, dry linoleum to protect the surface; Her Ladyship thinks this would quickly start to smell unpleasant and recommends those who wish to take the nostalgic route to opt for Mrs Beeton's other suggestion, 15g of shredded beeswax dissolved in a little turpentine, or to stick to a high-quality floor polish, such as that made by the National Trust.

A TIP FOR PROTECTING FLOORS

Whatever the surface, Her Ladyship recommends protective pads. Generally made of felt, these are readily and cheaply available from hardware shops and are designed to fit under the legs or corners of heavy furniture. They protect the floor from scuffs and scratches and reduce the indentations in carpet. For furniture with casters, buy caster cups, which may be brass, chrome or (if you must) plastic and are ideal for carpet; on wooden floors you'll also need the felt pads to sit under the cups.

Dusting

Almost all other household tasks raise dust, so if you are working through a list of tasks dusting should be done last.

There may well be instances in which less is more, but when it comes to dusting less is less. One Victorian expert on household management reckoned that it took 'a brisk girl' three hours to dust the average parlour, overcrowded as it was with the knick-knacks of the age. You, dear Reader, Her Ladyship ventures to suggest, have better things to do with your time. Possessing and displaying less 'stuff', unless you keep it in a glass cabinet, will cut your dusting time enormously. Remember also the maxim that ornaments that remain dusty remain whole. Display precious china on a high shelf and no one will notice that you haven't dusted it lately.

It should go without saying that dusters must always be clean: the object of the exercise is to remove dust, not move it from one place to another. On painted shelves and most of the surfaces in the kitchen and bathroom, a slightly damp cloth does a better job than a duster for this reason. Take dusters outside after each use and shake them thoroughly; you should also wash them frequently. Throw away any that develop raw edges or dangling threads – they are likely to catch on furniture and leave unsightly tufts. Keep dusters used for other purposes, such as polishing shoes or silver, separately so that you don't use them for dusting by mistake.

Removing each book from the shelf and dusting it daily is a task that belongs to the days of under-housemaids, but book lovers may like to do it occasionally. An old-fashioned shaving brush is a useful tool here, though if you are dealing with airport-bought reading material rather than rare first editions the 'dusting' may also be done with the soft brush attachment of the vacuum cleaner. Remove the jacket of a hardback to prevent damage, then hold the book upside down and firmly closed so that the dust does not drift down between the pages.

What sort of duster?

Purists recommend an extraordinary range of brushes for specific tasks: horsehair for removing cobwebs, goat hair for gentle polishing, pig bristles for the computer keyboard. All very well, says Her Ladyship, if you happen to live in a farmyard. Readily available micro-fibre cloths serve most purposes perfectly well – and do not cause colourful disasters in the washing machine as the old-fashioned yellow duster was prone to do. If you like natural fabrics and therefore prefer to stick to yellow dusters, buy the best possible quality: the cheaper the cloth, the more quickly it will start snagging on the furniture. Not even the best quality that Her Ladyship has discovered is colourfast, however, so be careful not to wash these dusters with anything lightly coloured.

Long-handled dusters are useful for lightshades, the tops of picture frames, dado rails, skirting boards and any other areas that would otherwise require stretching or bending, not to mention random spider's webs. Her Ladyship's is made of lamb's wool; ostrich feathers are also recommended and readily available. Alternatively, improvise by draping a duster over the end of a floor brush or a dry mop.

Suiting brushes to individual tasks is more important: they should be used for the job for which they are intended and nothing else. If you use a brush for cleaning silver, for example, mark it in some way that identifies it as the silver brush and don't use it to dust ceramics. Small paintbrushes are useful for the awkward bits on ornaments.

A TIP FOR DUSTING BLINDS
Lower them fully and brush with a damp paintbrush.

Polishing

…is, in Her Ladyship's view, an overrated activity that, taken to excess, can do more harm than good to wood surfaces. Applying a light and even coating of beeswax and rubbing it in thoroughly to produce an even shine builds up a protective surface that is easier to dust, but should be done no more than twice a year. Buffing a polished surface with a clean duster or chamois leather after dusting gives it all the enhancement it needs for most of the time.

The National Trust gives this advice about buffing:

> Polished surfaces, particularly those which are unavoidably touched, such as doors and banisters, may need occasional buffing with a soft, clean duster or chamois leather to remove fingermarks and revive the shine… Before buffing, remove dust from the surface to prevent scratches. Then fold the cloth into a soft pad to fit the palm of one hand, making sure that there are no loose threads or edges which could catch on the woodwork. Apply just enough pressure to remove fingermarks and revive the lustre; too much pressure can result in a streaky surface… Always finish buffing in the direction of the grain.

The advice about folding the cloth into a pad applies to all cleaning cloths as a way of ensuring that there are no rough edges to catch or scratch surfaces. To quote the National Trust again, 'Lay the cloth flat and fold the four corners into the centre, then do the same with the four corners now created. Turn this over and you will have a soft smooth pad.'

If a wooden banister has become really grimy, buffing may not be enough. Dampen (but do not saturate – you don't want it to drip) a clean soft cloth or cotton wool swabs with warm water containing a little detergent and wipe a small area at a time. Rinse immediately, then dry with a cotton duster. Make sure this duster is completely dry – change it as soon as it is damp. If you want to wax the banister to restore a shine, leave it to dry out overnight first.

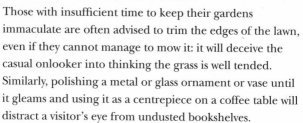

WHAT THE EYE DOESN'T SEE...

Those with insufficient time to keep their gardens
immaculate are often advised to trim the edges of the lawn,
even if they cannot manage to mow it: it will deceive the
casual onlooker into thinking the grass is well tended.
Similarly, polishing a metal or glass ornament or vase until
it gleams and using it as a centrepiece on a coffee table will
distract a visitor's eye from undusted bookshelves.

Cleaning leather

Dusting leather chairs and sofas should be part of the weekly
routine; once a year they should be cleaned more thoroughly.
For antique leather, the National Trust suggests removing
'tackiness' with a cotton cloth and a little white spirit, and
recommends nothing heavier than buffing to restore a shine. In
the domestic context, you will not harm a leather sofa if you use
a proprietary leather cleaner: rub into the surface with a soft cloth,
then apply a leather protection cream to feed and condition the
leather and help minimise wear and tear. Avoid sitting on the
furniture for twenty-four hours, then polish to a shine with a clean,
soft duster.

This treatment may also be used on desktops and other
leather surfaces (not to mention handbags), but take care not to
allow products designed for leather to spill over on to the
surrounding wood.

CHAMOIS LEATHER

Very effective used dry for buffing (see page 25) or slightly damp for windows, mirrors and the car, chamois – sheepskin treated with fish oil – can absorb up to six times its weight in water. It is also wonderfully soft, so it doesn't scratch surfaces. Her Ladyship would advocate buying the real thing in preference to a cheaper synthetic substitute.

If you use it damp, rinse it thoroughly in warm water afterwards, then rub it with soap and work up a lather. Rinse again, soap again and squeeze dry. Without rinsing this time, allow the cloth to dry away from direct heat, fold it and put it away. Before using it again, rinse thoroughly and squeeze dry. The soap will have kept it soft and supple.

Protecting furniture

Nowadays not many of us abandon our town house or country house for several months of the year, so 'closing down' and draping the furniture in Holland covers is no longer necessary. The 'polite' covers once in everyday use to protect furniture so that its expensive upholstery was displayed only on special occasions would now be deemed rather impolite, and the antimacassars used to prevent a chair back being smeared with a man's hair oil have a Victorian quaintness that is not everyone's choice of 'look'. However, a few simple measures can be adopted to minimise wear and tear on furniture.

First of all, protect it from too much direct sunlight. Upholstery fades quickly in bright light, so position precious furniture away from a sunny window. To give an heirloom extra protection, you may like to install UV film on your windows, but in most homes Her Ladyship would feel this was overkill.

Move furniture occasionally to spread the wear. If you are a four-person household which owns eight dining chairs, rotate them so that the same four are not used day in and day out, leaving four of them pristine when the others need to be refurbished. Similarly, if you live alone and own two comfortable chairs but always sit in the same one, move them around every few months so that although you are still sitting in your favourite place, you are giving equal wear to both chairs.

Eco-cleaning

Her Ladyship believes that her readers' relationship with the planet is their own business and is certainly beyond the scope of this book. Proprietary products for all imaginable forms of cleaning are available in every supermarket and hardware shop; for many there are now 'eco-friendly' variations which purport to minimise impact on the environment. It is Her Ladyship's experience that some of these products are more effective than others and that, for the eco-conscious, many household tasks can be performed very efficiently with lemon juice, clear vinegar or baking or washing soda.

The only area in which she would express a strong opinion is that of dusting, buffing and polishing. As is mentioned elsewhere in this chapter, dusting and buffing should be frequent activities; polishing with beeswax need be done only sparingly. Proprietary aerosol polishes or any polishing products that contain silicone or cellulose have no place in Her Ladyship's home.

Her Ladyship is no great believer in throws. She thinks that you buy a chair or sofa because you like it; it is a shame to cover it up to prevent it getting dirty. However, there is no denying that throws are easier to wash than armchairs and they are one solution to the 'wear and tear' problem. In households with a full complement of children, dogs and accompanying mud and biscuit crumbs, they save a lot of work, and can make a 'tired but comfortable' piece of furniture look fresher until you have energy and budget to replace it.

Cleaning windows and mirrors

Window sills and frames may be dusted or vacuumed. For the glass or mirror itself, brush or dust off the worst of the dirt, then wipe with a damp chamois leather (see the box on page 27) and dry with a soft cotton cloth or a plastic-bladed window wiper. For stubborn dirt use a very little washing-up liquid or vinegar in warm water. Drying with newspaper or paper towels also works: the important thing is that whatever you use for drying must be absolutely dry. One Victorian manual recommends rubbing with 'hot, strong vinegar' to remove paint marks from glass; and if you have access to industrial methylated spirits or distilled or de-ionized water, they work wonders too.

For stained glass or small panes of leaded glass, cotton-wool swabs will give you access to tricky corners.

Clean the glass on paintings and photographs with a damp cloth. Don't spray with an aerosol cleaner, as this may seep behind the glass and damage the picture.

Cleaning silver

The 'stitch in time' approach prevents this from becoming a major chore. Try to do it once a month or so.

Once upon a time, silver was always wrapped in felt and this is still the best way of storing it; fabric bags or acid-free paper are satisfactory alternatives. Never wrap silver in newspaper, which contains acid and will damage it. Never use rubber bands to hold a set of cutlery together, as they too will cause damage.

When cleaning, first remove surface grease by rubbing gently with a cloth dampened in distilled water. Remove any remaining tarnish by rubbing – again gently; the gentle touch is very important for silver – with an impregnated silver-cleaning cloth. A soft brush or cotton bud dipped in silver dip is useful for reaching into the whorls of ornate patterns. Finally, rub the tarnish-free item again with spirit to remove any lingering marks and/or wash it in hot soapy water and dry it immediately. Use silver dip only on

DO ONE, GET ONE FREE

The comedian George Burns, famous for his longevity, is quoted as saying, 'You know you're getting old when you stoop to tie your shoelaces and wonder what else you could do while you're down there.' Her Ladyship believes that this attitude can usefully be applied to housework, whatever your age. If, for example, you have high ceilings and need a stepladder to change a light bulb, clean the lampshades and the difficult-to-reach top shelves while you are up there. If you have the silver polish out to clean the cutlery, rub the cloth over metal door handles as well. This way, you'll find you have done two or three useful jobs when you set out to do only one.

a suitable work surface: spilling even a small quantity on the dining table will make a distressing and long-lasting mess.

The majority of tarnishing comes from exposure to heat. This is why wooden spoons find a place in the most aristocratic of kitchens: no self-respecting cook would ever stir hot food with a silver utensil. A tip courtesy of the experts at the Victoria and Albert Museum: egg yolk is another culprit when it comes to tarnishing (it is for this reason that egg spoons were once frequently made of horn when all other cutlery was silver). If you use silver spoons for eggs at the breakfast table, wash them (in hot soapy water, not the dishwasher) and dry them immediately; then, if necessary, polish them with a silver cloth.

A finishing touch

Flowers brighten any home, not only when guests are expected. The subject of flower arranging is too vast to go into in detail here, but a few basic tips may not go amiss.

Before arranging flowers, remove foliage from the lower part of the stem. Any leaves left under the water when you arrange them will rot. Cut woody stems such as roses at a sharp angle and then cut about 1cm up the middle of each stem. Do not crush them, as this damages the plant tissues and reduces the life expectancy of the plant. Cut softer stems at a similar angle; with bulbs such as daffodils and tulips, make sure that you remove any firm, white part at the base of the stems.

Place your flowers in a bucket about a quarter full of warm water to which you have added flower food (usually supplied by florists). With bulbs, use cold water unless you want the flowers to open quickly. Leave for at least two hours, preferably overnight.

When arranging, make sure that your tallest flowers are at least twice as high as your vase. Put taller flowers at the back, if the arrangement is to stand against a wall, or centre, if it is to be the centrepiece of a table, with smaller ones (or smaller pieces of foliage) to the front and sides. If necessary, chop a bit off some stems so that not all the plants are the same height. Similarly, if some of your flowers are in bud and others in full bloom, put the full blooms at the back or centre. If you have flowers of different colours, make sure that they are arranged to produce a balanced, pleasing look: don't have all the red ones on one side and all the white on another unless you specifically want your arrangement to conjure up images of a rugby match.

Fill but do not overfill a vase with flowers. Too many flowers will look cramped and be difficult to arrange elegantly; too few will look sparse and will flop unbecomingly. Fill the vase about three-quarters full with tepid water (neither very warm nor stone cold) and add more flower food. Change the water and add more food every three days or so (more often if it starts to look dirty).

An alternative to a conventional vase is any water-tight container in which you have placed a substantial piece of flower foam (often known by the trade name Oasis). The foam should reach a centimetre or so above the container to allow your arrangement to flow over it. Soak the piece of foam for 20 minutes before using and insert the flower stems into it individually. Don't press them all the way through – the base of each stem should be inside the foam. Do not on any account allow the foam to dry out. Check it daily and water it as required. Flower foam is also the ideal medium for a dried flower arrangement and the same basic design rules apply.

Flower arranging without tears

When arranging flowers anywhere that drips might damage the flooring, cover the floor area with a sheet of polythene. Lift the polythene as soon as you have finished, being careful not to let water or the odd bit of pollen fall on to the carpet, thus rendering the whole exercise pointless. Once the arrangement is done, stand the vase on a waterproof mat or a saucer to avoid staining the furniture underneath when you water. If you don't have attractive waterproof mats, use a table mat made of cork or some other hard material and cover it with a pretty and washable cloth. Do the same with house plants. Position your arrangement away from draughts, direct heat or strong sunlight.

Lily pollen gets everywhere and makes an orange stain on carpet, tables and clothes that is difficult to remove. To avoid this, pull the pollen-bearing stamens off with your fingers (this gives a better-looking finish than if you use scissors) while they are still lying on the paper or cellophane in which they were delivered. Wrap the debris carefully. If the pollen does get on clothes, do not be tempted to dab at it with a damp cloth. Instead, remove as much as possible with sticky tape, treat with a pre-wash stain remover, then wash at the highest temperature the fabric will tolerate.

The bedroom

The previous advice on dusting and vacuuming covers most of the needs of the living areas, but applies equally to bedrooms. Here, in addition to weekly 'maintenance', the following tasks should be performed at least every month or so:

• **Vacuum under the bed**, if you haven't had the foresight to buy one with drawers that go down to floor level (see Her Ladyship's thoughts on storage, page 15–16). This requires a vacuum cleaner with a long, flexible hose. Move anything that is being stored under the bed – it is extraordinary what long-lost treasures this may bring to light – and tuck the bedspread or any hanging covers out of the way. Use the main vacuum-cleaner head for most of the area and switch to a small brush or crevice attachment for the legs, baseboard and nooks and crannies. There is no avoiding doing some of this task on your hands and knees, so you may choose to delegate it shamelessly to a younger and more agile member of your household.

• **Turn the mattress** if this is what the manufacturers recommend. Some modern mattresses have a warm side and a cool side, so should be turned upside down according to season; others are designed in such a way that turning is unnecessary. All should, however, be rotated through 180° (that is, keep the same side up, but put the head to the foot and vice versa) to ensure even wear.

• **Vacuum or brush the mattress.** Again, follow the manufacturers' instructions. Vacuuming is often recommended as the best way to ensure the bed is mite-free, but the manufacturers of Her Ladyship's mattress warn that this will damage the filling and recommend brushing instead.

• **On a fine day, take pillows and duvets outside** and leave them for about two hours to air.

See Chapter 4 for Her Ladyship's advice on bed linen.

The kitchen

Because you are preparing food in it, the kitchen is the room in which cleanliness is paramount. Work surfaces should be immaculately clean: wipe them down every day and every time you prepare a meal: use a cloth dampened in warm water and a bit of washing-up liquid or proprietary cleaner. Wipe up spillages (on floor, counter top, hob or anywhere else) immediately – this is real 'stitch in time' territory. Wipe the microwave down frequently, inside and out, not forgetting the turntable. Loosen any stubborn food spills by heating a cup of water in the microwave first. Keep any appliances that sit on kitchen surfaces (toaster, kettle, electric mixer, knife block, etc) clean. Empty and clean the toaster's crumb tray every day or two if you make a lot of toast and every week or so if you don't.

Empty and clean the toaster's crumb tray every day or two if you make a lot of toast and every week or so if you don't.

Never leave the washing up to accumulate for days. And perform the more arduous tasks described below often enough to prevent them becoming even more arduous than they need to be.

Kitchen gadgetry

What you need in the kitchen depends entirely on how much cooking you do and what form it takes. Her Ladyship does not possess a microwave, but understands that it is indispensable to those who need to heat up or defrost in a hurry. Many people also swear by food processors; Her Ladyship does perfectly well without one and instead relies on an electric hand whisk and a sturdily built liquidiser, which is excellent for turning left-over vegetables into soup.

However if, like Her Ladyship, you are a lover of cook shops, your kitchen is likely to be full of gadgets that you literally never use – extravagances that seemed like a good idea at the time. Into this category Her Ladyship would put olive pitters, mango slicers and pineapple corers: olives can be bought ready pitted and there is little the other devices can achieve that a sharp knife cannot.

There are, however, three comparative luxuries that Her Ladyship would not be without:

• **A steamer.** Not only is steaming one of the healthiest ways of cooking vegetables, but stacking three layers one on top of the other is a great saver of space on the hob.

• **A herb knife.** Those half-moon-shaped double-handled choppers really do work, and stop you cutting the tips of your fingers off.

• **A meat thermometer** – the easy way to tell whether beef is as rare as you like it or when meats that should not be underdone, such as poultry, are cooked through.

In the long term, it is much more rewarding to spend your money on good-quality equipment for daily tasks than on fripperies you will rarely use. With saucepans, baking and roasting tins, casseroles and knives in particular, always buy the best you can afford. Weight is a good test of quality here: although opinions vary about the respective merits of cast iron (extremely heavy) and hard-anodised aluminium (lighter, but still very solid) saucepans, what they have in common is that they are hard-wearing, distribute heat evenly and don't conduct it so quickly that food burns the moment your back is turned. If you have an induction hob, you are probably aware that certain types of pan cannot be used on it, so buy carefully.

Sturdiness is important in most kitchenware. Her Ladyship advocates buying this in person rather than online, so that you can feel the weight and, with knives, potato peelers and the like, check that they sit comfortably in your hand.

SHARPENING KNIVES

Knives are useless and dangerous if they are not kept sharp. The best way to sharpen them is with a steel, but this requires practice and manual dexterity. A safer alternative for the awkward-of-hand is a knife sharpener: it sits on the kitchen work surface and you run the blade through it a few times without endangering your fingers. Make sure that the knife is clean before using the sharpener: even little bits of grease may gum up the works and make it less efficient.

A note about shopping

This is another aspect of domestic life to which you should not become a slave. Work out a system that suits you, whether it is taking the car to a huge supermarket once a week and doing everything in one fell swoop or walking to the shops and buying little and often. Alternatively, if shopping to keep your household fed is an albatross around the neck of every Saturday morning, have groceries delivered. This is not an extravagance – for a working woman it is money well spent, as it liberates her to do something she would rather be doing, or to earn the money to pay for it. A compromise is to have cumbersome, non-perishable items such as breakfast cereals and washing-up liquid delivered, leaving you with time and energy to support your local fruit and vegetable or farmers' market, butcher, fishmonger and delicatessen when it comes to fresh food.

Washing dishes

Not everything can be washed by machine. Wooden-, bone- or ivory-handled knives, for example, will be ruined; silver is fine, as long as it does not come in contact with stainless steel. Her Ladyship's steamer and non-stick pans came with instructions that they should be washed by hand; she also chooses not to entrust tall-stemmed wine glasses to the dishwasher, though she is aware that many people do.

The traditional advice about washing by hand is still valid today. Scrape any leftovers into the bin before you start – don't contaminate your washing-up water with an unwanted slice of lemon or sprig of parsley. Start with the items that are least dirty. That usually means glasses, followed by cutlery, crockery, mixing bowls and other 'preparing' utensils, then finally pans. Use very hot water (so hot that you need to wear rubber gloves) and change it as soon as it begins to look less than

WASHING-UP LIQUID…
…is a much undervalued commodity. In addition to the purpose for which it was created, it may be squirted into bath water to prevent scum forming round the bath; used to clean spots off carpets; and rubbed (sparingly) on windows and mirrors to prevent condensation.

fresh and the bubbles from the washing-up liquid look tired.

Glasses and any silver items should be dried (preferably immediately) and rubbed to a shine with a clean, dry cloth. For everything else, rinsing in very hot water and then leaving to drain is more hygienic.

'Every now and then' tasks: defrosting the freezer

Nowadays many ovens are self-cleaning; many freezers and almost all refrigerators are self-defrosting. Those that are not need regular maintenance to keep them functioning efficiently.

Defrost the freezer before ice has built up over the 'ceiling' and all the bags have frozen together. This may be as little as once a year or as frequently as every two to three months. A build-up of about 1cm of ice shows that the time has come.

Before defrosting, reduce the contents to a minimum by eating them. The real purposes of this are to dispose of unlabelled packages that may otherwise linger at the base of the freezer for years, and to minimise the amount of food that has to be kept cold while the defrosting is going on. However, it should also be enjoyed as an exercise in itself, as it produces some highly imaginative meals. Her Ladyship has fond memories of a prawn with vegetable chilli *en croûte* that she has never since been able to reconstruct.

When you come to defrost, wrap any food left in the freezer in several layers of newspaper or plastic and put it in the fridge or an insulated coolbox of the kind you take on picnics. Turn the freezer off. Put pans or bowls of hot water inside to hasten the defrosting process and line the base of the freezer with tea towels or other similar cloths to absorb the water. As the ice softens, remove it by hand or with the aid of a plastic spatula (not metal, as that will damage the surface of the freezer walls). Warming the ice with a hand-held hairdryer is often recommended as a way of making it melt more quickly but, as the purpose of defrosting a freezer is to make it more energy-efficient, Her Ladyship is inclined to frown upon this wanton use of electricity, not to mention that water and hairdryers don't mix well. She advises her readers to spend an hour with a good book while letting nature take its course.

When all the ice has melted – which may take up to three or four hours if there is a lot of it – wipe the insides of the freezer dry with a clean cloth. Switch the freezer on again and allow it to cool to near its normal temperature before replacing the food.

A NOTE ABOUT FREEZING

Never, ever put anything in the freezer unlabelled. In the fridge this matters less, as you are likely to use up leftovers in a matter of days and therefore more likely to remember what they were. With the freezer, months may elapse before you decide to defrost and eat whatever it may be, memory plays strange tricks and you don't want to be pouring what you thought was raspberry coulis over ice cream only to discover that it is borsch.

Cleaning the fridge

Doing this once a month is a hygienic practice in itself, but also a useful way of discovering anything past its 'best before' date that may be lurking in the deep recesses. Turn the fridge off. Remove all the food and wipe any drips of jam or mayonnaise from jars. Throw out anything that is about to start walking round the fridge on its own. Remove removable drawers and racks and wash them in the sink in hot, soapy water. Rinse and leave to dry.

Clean the inside of the fridge with hot, soapy water (washing-up liquid is ideal) and a soft cloth or sponge (not a scouring pad, as this will damage surfaces). Wipe everything thoroughly, removing odd bits of food from corners and not forgetting any unremovable trays or compartments, nor the grooves into which the racks fit. Rinse with warm water. As a precaution against odours, it is worth wiping again, this time with a solution of baking soda: about 2 tablespoons dissolved in a litre of warm water gives the right strength. Restore the removable parts and the food to their proper places and switch the fridge back on.

If something malodorous has left its mark and this cleaning routine doesn't remove the smell, empty the fridge but leave it switched on. Spread a few tablespoons of ground coffee on a plate (or two or more if necessary) and leave it in the fridge without opening the door for 24–48 hours. Then throw away the coffee, but keep an open packet in the fridge to prevent a recurrence of the problem. Her Ladyship recommends cheap coffee for this purpose: it is serving purely as a deodoriser. The better-quality coffee that you intend to drink should be kept sealed.

The bad news: if the odour is in the insulation, none of the above is likely to remove it. The insulation will probably have to be replaced. Prevention, as elsewhere in this book, is better (and cheaper) than cure.

Cleaning the oven

The parts to clean vary from make to make and manufacturers' instructions should always be followed. Usually, however, you clean the base and the sides but not the top. Readily available spray-on chemical products are effective but caustic: wear rubber gloves, line the floor with plenty of newspaper (and have plenty more on hand for when this needs to be changed) and make sure the kitchen is well ventilated. Follow the instructions on the tin meticulously.

A less toxic but time-consuming alternative is to use bicarbonate of soda on a cold oven. Again wearing rubber gloves, cover the area to be to cleaned with a layer of bicarbonate of soda about 5mm thick. Using a spray bottle such as you might use to moisten the leaves of house plants, spray the soda until it is quite damp, but not saturated. Leave for an hour or so. As the soda begins to dry out, spray it again. Repeat three or four times, then, using a rubber or plastic spatula or a sponge, scrape the soda away and the food residue should come away with it. Rinse the oven thoroughly with cold water.

To make the task easier next time, invest in a large baking sheet to line the bottom of the oven. Remove it and wash it whenever it looks as if it needs it. Alternatively, line the base of the oven with a smooth sheet of aluminium foil. When it is dirty, throw it away and replace.

If all this sounds just too much, there are oven-cleaning specialists who will do the job for you. They'll also take on the extractor hood, the AGA, the microwave and various other cookery-related appliances that may have become covered with a daunting quantity of grease and grime.

Limescale in the kettle

A perpetual problem in hard-water areas, a build-up of limescale will make the kettle less efficient, use more electricity and shorten the appliance's life. It's best to deal with it regularly. As a preventive, the traditional remedy of keeping a few shells in the kettle to act as an abrasive is still effective. Any shells will do: in Victorian times flat oyster shells were recommended because in those days oysters were cheap and ubiquitous, not because the oyster had unique lime-breaking powers.

> *As a preventive, the traditional remedy of keeping a few shells in the kettle to act as an abrasive is still effective.*

For a more thorough clean, cover the element and any other affected areas with a mixture of one part water to one part white vinegar. If the encrustation is severe, increase the proportion of vinegar. Do not boil the kettle at this stage. Leave overnight, or at least for a few hours. When you discard the water most of the limescale should come away with it. Any lingering remnants should be soft enough to be removed with an old toothbrush or even a finger. Rinse the kettle. Then, most important: fill it with clean water, boil it up and *discard this water* to remove the aroma of vinegar.

As an alternative to vinegar use lemon juice – about 2 tablespoons to half a kettleful of water – boil, then rinse thoroughly.

The bathroom

The frequent use of proprietary products will keep the bathroom in a reasonable state of cleanliness. But be sure to clean everything – don't ignore the undersides or bases of the basin and loo, or the underside of the loo seat. More challenging are accumulations of limescale round taps and soap scum on shower doors or curtains.

For limescale, again there are proprietary products that will do the job, but they come with frightening cautions on the container. Wear rubber gloves, use in a well-ventilated space and follow the manufacturer's instructions to the letter.

A less fierce and more environmentally friendly option is to scrub with a mixture of half clear vinegar, half water, using a soft toothbrush. Don't use undiluted vinegar, as it may damage the enamel surface of bath or basin. Rinse well and dry with a soft cloth. If this isn't enough, soak a cloth in the diluted vinegar and wrap it round the tap. Leave for an hour, then rinse, scrape off any loose scale with a toothbrush and dry as before.

Soap scum on glass, tiles and chrome can be removed with a paste made from clear vinegar and baking soda: wipe it on with a cloth or sponge, leave for a few minutes, then rinse and buff dry. Keeping a plastic-bladed window wiper in the shower and encouraging everyone to wipe the shower cubicle or screen down after each use helps keep soap scum to a minimum.

Most shower curtains are machine washable; adding a tablespoon of washing soda crystals to the detergent will help remove the stubborn stains that build up on the bottom of the curtain. Alternatively, soak it in the bath in warm water containing a washing-machine-load quantity of detergent and two or three tablespoons of washing soda.

TIPS ABOUT LIMESCALE

Drying the taps, bath and basin after each use helps prevent the build-up of limescale. Also, hot water calcifies (turns into lime) more readily than cold, so rinse the shower head etc. with cold water.

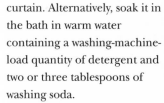

Grouting that started life as a brilliant white will inevitably dim with the passage of time. Clean it as you would any other part of the bathroom but, to minimise the work, do it immediately after someone has taken a hot shower: the steam will loosen dirt.

Cheering up the bathroom

Depending on the size of the room, there are various things you can do to prevent a bathroom from being the dreariest place in the house. Many plants that would wilt in a centrally heated living room will thrive in a bathroom's humidity. Be warned, however: ferns and weeping figs may enjoy the atmosphere so much that your bathroom turns into a jungle; a more restrained and elegant orchid may be a better choice.

Most people prefer to keep all but the most frequently used toiletries such as toothpaste and shampoo in a cabinet (and certainly anything remotely intimate, including medication, should be out of sight when guests are expected), but displays of glass bottles containing coloured cotton wool, bath salts and the like can sit very prettily on a spare shelf or two-tiered table.

Books and humidity, of course, do not go well together, so if you do choose to keep some in the bathroom, make sure that there is nothing precious among them. In a separate WC, where humidity levels are less of an issue, a shelf of 'loo books' can be fun: the concern here is not to put in anything so engrossing that readers will occupy the room to the discomfort of other members of the household.

All this said, anyone who has read the earlier parts of this chapter will be aware that Her Ladyship has an aversion to 'stuff'. Any form of ornament in the bathroom must be kept clean if it is to be appealing to the eye, so lovers of talcum powder may decide that ornaments are all too much like hard work.

Outside the house

Even if there is little or no garden involved, pride in your home should extend beyond the front door. As a regular part of the housekeeping routine, and particularly when you are expecting visitors, sweep the approach to the house and trim any dead foliage off the pot plant on the doorstep. In Her Ladyship's view a scruffy adornment is appreciably less attractive than no adornment at all. Allowing the front yard, even of a communal property, to become a repository for old washing machines, discarded mattresses or rusty motorcycles is a solecism comparable to keeping a bicycle in the hallway – to be avoided at all costs.

Sharing the load

It is a well-known fact that most men have a higher 'mess threshold' than most women and have to be reminded that housework needs to be done. A (female) friend of Her Ladyship's once told a tale of vacuuming her living room one Saturday while her (male) partner sat reading the paper. He looked up, glanced round the room apparently oblivious to what she was doing and remarked, 'This flat keeps itself quite clean, doesn't it?' An extreme example, perhaps, but not an atypical one.

Most couples sooner or later find a form of demarcation that is remarkably similar to the one used by their parents and grandparents: she does most of the housework and cooking, he looks after the car, the garden and basic maintenance. These gender-specific roles are no longer cast in stone, however, and many women are every bit as handy with a spanner or a paintbrush as their male partners are with a saucepan. The point is that – assuming both members of the partnership work – you must come to an amicable arrangement about the sharing of chores.

One way around this problem is 'timesharing'. Say you have an antipathy to dust and choose to spend fifteen minutes every three days doing the dusting. Someone else in your household may not care two hoots about dust, but be willing to spend two hours a month cleaning the windows. Thus you both contribute approximately the same amount of time, you agree always to do the dusting, your companion agrees always to clean the windows and you both avoid the perpetual 'Why is it always me who does…?' argument.

This system, however, works only if it is mutually agreed and all concerned stick to it. A woman (or a houseproud man living with someone less houseproud of whichever gender) who deliberately neglects the housework in the hope that, sooner or later, her partner will notice and get out the vacuum cleaner must resign herself to living with unvacuumed carpets. In many households there seems, sadly, to be no way round the necessity for what men call nagging and women call asking him for the hundredth time.

Whatever your partner's defects in terms of domesticity, it is almost certain that if you have teenage children they will be many times worse. The busy mother who says, 'Oh for heaven's sake, I'll do it myself' or simply accepts that her fifteen-year-old's bedroom is a health hazard is saving herself a lot of grief. However, there is a new area of family dynamics that needs to be sorted out in the interests of harmony for all concerned: the one involving adult offspring, perhaps back from university and not yet able to afford a place of their own, living at home.

> ***Whatever your partner's defects in terms of domesticity, it is almost certain that if you have teenage children they will be many times worse.***

Although it really falls outside the remit of this book, and without feeling equipped to give definitive answers to these questions, Her Ladyship recommends that ground rules are established on the subjects of:

• **Paying rent** or making a contribution to household expenses.

• **Having meals with the parents.** Is it reasonable to expect a twenty-four-year-old to tell her mother whether or not she will be home for dinner? Answer, in Her Ladyship's view: yes, categorically, if she is expecting her mother to cook for her. One friend whose back-at-home son works long hours has come to the perfectly satisfactory arrangement that she *doesn't* expect him for dinner unless he tells her otherwise.

• **Raiding the fridge.** While you probably don't want to insist on a 'yours' and 'mine' shelf as you might have done in student days, you equally don't want to come home from work to find that what you had planned to cook for supper has been laid waste by the unemployed twenty-something who has been home all day.

• **Visitors.** How many at a time is acceptable and where (and with whom) do they sleep?

After that, Her Ladyship feels she can add only, 'Good luck.'

PAYING YOUR CHILDREN
Even grown-up children respond to bribery. Her Ladyship recommends paying them a weekly sum to perform a specified list of household tasks. Make it roughly equivalent to the money you would give them anyway to ensure that they took a taxi home after a late night out and consider the housework as a return on your investment.

Two

HOUSEHOLD
EMERGENCIES

*The following is a good method of removing stains from ivory: wash
it well in soap and water, and place it, while wet, in the sunshine.
Wash it several times in the same way for two or three days, keeping
it in the sun, and it will soon become beautifully white.*

'Isobel' of *Home Notes: Things a Woman Wants to Know,* c. 1900

Her Ladyship is not sure that this is practical advice for the keys of
her late grandmother's piano, and many age-old tips for cleaning,
polishing and stain removing require modern-day interpretation.
The same source suggests renewing the colours in a carpet by
sponging it with a solution of one part ox-gall to two parts water,
and cleaning mother-of-pearl by washing it with powdered whiting
and cold water. Her Ladyship confesses freely that she doesn't
want even to think about what ox-gall is and can only assume that
the whiting referred to here is not a fish.

Many traditional methods are still valid – and less daunting
than those just mentioned – but most of the stain-removing
techniques offered in this brief chapter have a slightly more
modern edge. It is therefore worth noting that they are perhaps a
little rough and ready for those whose furniture is made by
Chippendale or Sheraton or whose carpets originate in Aubusson.
In these circumstances, the National Trust recommends scraping
up solids and blotting liquids, then keeping the stain damp with a

poultice until expert help arrives. Her Ladyship would add that if you own this sort of furniture or carpet it is prudent to keep the relevant experts' numbers in your iPhone.

The most important rule is that all spillages should be cleared up as soon as possible after the event. If the spillage is food, scoop up as much as possible using a spoon or spatula before tackling the resulting stain. For blotting, always use white paper towels or white absorbent cloths that you don't mind getting dirty. Blotting a stain on a white linen tablecloth with a white linen napkin merely transfers and prolongs the damage.

Note: unless otherwise stated, all the cleaning described in this chapter uses cold or lukewarm water; hot water is likely to set a stain (particularly in the case of blood) and make it difficult or impossible to remove completely.

Removing common household stains

White wine: rinse with cold water, from the back if possible. Rub with washing-up liquid and leave for 5–7 minutes. Rinse thoroughly. If the stain is still visible, rub again with washing-up liquid and soak in cold water for half an hour. Rinse again. If the stain is on a garment, napkin or table cloth, rub or spray with a spot-stain remover before washing.

Red wine: blot immediately with white paper towels or other white absorbent material. Sponge gently with soda water, or warm water in which you have dissolved a teaspoonful of bicarbonate of soda. Repeat if necessary. Don't sprinkle it with salt, as this is likely to set the stain. Attempting to remove red wine by soaking it with white wine is, in Her Ladyship's view, simply wasteful: once it has soaked for a while, it still needs to be thoroughly rinsed, so why not do the soaking with soda water and drink the white wine while you are waiting for it to take effect?

Blood: blot immediately with a white cloth dampened with cold water. Rinse the cloth and blot again. If the stain persists, add a squirt of neutral detergent to a cup of lukewarm water and use this to blot again. With blood it is particularly important not to rub and not to use hot water.

Coffee, tea or chocolate: blot immediately to absorb as much of the liquid as possible. Work from the outside inwards to avoid spreading the stain. Add a squirt of washing-up liquid to a couple of cups of lukewarm water, sponge the stain gently and blot again. Then make up a solution of two parts lukewarm water to one part white vinegar, sponge the area again and blot with a clean white cloth or kitchen towels. Rinse and blot again.

Fruit juice: blot immediately to absorb as much of the juice as possible. Then either dab the stain with a damp sponge or squirt it with a little lukewarm water; in either case, use only enough water to make the carpet or material damp rather than sodden. Blot again with paper towels and if necessary repeat the process. If a stain on carpet persists, add about 5ml of washing-up liquid or gentle carpet shampoo to a cup of water. Dampen a clean cloth with this liquid and lay it over the stain. Using the back of a spoon, rub the cloth gently in a swirling motion, working from the outside of the stain to the centre. Remove the cloth and dab the stain with paper towels until there is no colour left in the liquid they are absorbing. Place a clean dry cloth over the damp patch, cover it with a piece of plastic and weigh it down with something heavy such as a book or full gin bottle (if the latter, lie it on its side so that it presses down on as much of the affected area as possible. Gin bottles are recommended because many of them are square-sided and won't roll around. If your drinks cabinet contains Cointreau – as, purely by chance, Her Ladyship's does – this makes an excellent alternative). Leave for a few hours and, when the cloth is removed, the carpet underneath should be clean.

Grease: Mrs Beeton recommended a paste made from magnesia and fuller's earth, but Her Ladyship suggests that bicarbonate of soda is a more accessible option nowadays. Dissolve enough of it in a little lukewarm water to make a paste. Apply to the stain, leave for half an hour, then soak in warm water with a little mild detergent. Then, if whatever is stained will go in the washing machine, break the 'no hot water' rule by washing at the highest temperature recommended for the fabric. For a greasy stain on carpet, cover with a sheet of thick brown paper and place a hot iron on it. The grease will seep through the paper; replace with another sheet and repeat until the paper comes away clean.

A TIP FOR REMOVING CANDLE WAX

First freeze it. If the item is small enough, put it in the freezer for half to three-quarters of an hour; if not, cover the affected areas with blocks of ice (keep them in plastic bags so that they do not flow all over the place when they melt). Much of the wax can then be chipped away using a rubber spatula.

Then melt it. Cover the remaining wax with kitchen towels and heat it with a hand-held hairdryer. As the wax melts, it will stick to the paper towel and the surface can then be wiped clean. Alternatively, spread a sheet of thin white blotting paper over the wax and iron it with the iron at its lowest setting.

Water: this can stain waxed or natural-finish furniture and floors. The best remedy is a lengthy one: rub the affected area with a small quantity of linseed oil (a household that owns a cricket bat should have a ready supply) and leave for up to a week. The wood should by then have reverted to its natural colour. If not, repeat and leave for another few days. Polish with beeswax to restore a shine. If speedier results are required, rub the stain with steel wool and apply a fresh coat of wax. If the stain persists, mix some salt into a little olive oil to produce a paste-like consistency, rub the paste over the stain and leave overnight. Wipe clean and re-wax.

A sporting problem

Grass stains on cricket whites? Add 2–3 tablespoons of washing soda to 2.5 litres of warm water (about 3cm in the bottom of an ordinary washing-up bowl) and soak for an hour or so. Rinse, then wash in the normal way. Alternatively, dab the grass stain with methylated spirits before washing.

Raspberry juice on the tennis shorts? Stains caused by dark red fruit or beetroot should be soaked in glycerine for half an hour, then rinsed. Alternatively, break the 'no hot water' rule: stretch the garment over the sink and pour hot water on it from a metre or so above. The success of this particular measure is attributed, by those better versed in the laws of physics than Her Ladyship, to a combination of height and friction.

Three

SPRING-CLEANING

The Mole had been working very hard all the morning, spring-cleaning his little home. First with brooms, then with dusters; then on ladders and steps and chairs, with a brush and a pail of whitewash; till he had dust in his throat and eyes, and splashes of whitewash all over his black fur, and an aching back and weary arms... It was small wonder, then, that he suddenly flung down his brush on the floor, said 'Bother!' and 'O blow!' and also 'Hang spring-cleaning!' and bolted out of the house without even waiting to put on his coat.

Kenneth Grahame, *The Wind in the Willows*, 1908

Her Ladyship has every sympathy with the Mole, and is grateful that spring-cleaning comes but once a year. She would also venture to point out that nowadays the Mole would probably have Health and Safety down on him like a ton of bricks, though that thought may not be entirely relevant here.

The idea behind spring-cleaning is that it freshens the home after the 'closed down' period of winter. Perhaps the embarrassed housewife used to feel that the return of sunshine would show up dirt that had been hidden during the dark days, though Her Ladyship is only too aware that a burst of bright winter sun settles unerringly on an undusted surface. In particular, spring-cleaning is traditionally regarded as an opportunity to dispose of clutter.

Her Ladyship recommends setting aside a weekend and just getting on with it, rather than picking items piecemeal off a 'to-do' list. The following is a suggested, but not necessarily an exhaustive, list of the tasks that might be performed during an annual blitz.

Although this regime is described as spring-cleaning, it is not compulsory to wait for spring to perform any of these tasks. Should the curtains look dirty or fingerprints appear on a picture frame at other times of the year, by all means clean them. But keep them on the spring-cleaning list and who knows? Perhaps, in a fit of equinoctial enthusiasm, you will feel like cleaning them again.

All rooms

Wash down ceilings and walls and thoroughly clean anything that is actually dirty (splashes of food in the kitchen, marks on walls made by sticky fingers or by knocking something against them). A paste made from dissolving bicarbonate of soda in a little warm water is useful here. Be gentle with wallpaper: it should never be more than damp and should not be scrubbed. For persistent stains it may be better to choose a commercial product suitable for your type of wallpaper, but see the box on page 60 for a nineteenth-century suggestion, and call in a specialist if in any doubt about your own competence.

In this overall cleaning programme, include easily overlooked areas such as doors, door handles, light fittings, air vents and switch plates.

Include easily overlooked areas such as doors, door handles, light fittings, air vents and switch plates.

In living areas and bedrooms this should not be an arduous task; it may be harder work in the kitchen if grease has been allowed to accumulate.

Take down net or lace curtains, remove hooks and rings and wash the curtains gently by hand (or according to manufacturers' instructions). When drying, remove from the drier or line before they are completely dry – the ironing required will be minimal. Wash or dry-clean other curtains. Check the care instructions particularly carefully, as washing curtains that should be dry-cleaned can result in shrinkage, colour running and other disasters. It can also destroy or diminish fire-retardant properties in the fabric.

Her Ladyship has a deep-rooted aversion to Venetian blinds, but her aversion becomes all the deeper if they are dirty. Take them down and wash them in hot soapy water – the bath tub is ideal, as you can then use the shower attachment to rinse them. Be very careful handling Venetian blinds, as the edges can cause vicious cuts.

A TIP FOR CLEANING WALLPAPER

Her Ladyship would still recommend this method of cleaning fingermarks from wallpaper, discovered in a book called *A New System of Domestic Cookery*, published in 1807:

> *First blow off the dust with the bellows. Divide a white loaf of eight days old into eight parts. Take the crust into your hand, and beginning at the top of the paper, wipe it downwards in the lightest manner with the crumb. Don't cross nor go upwards. The dirt of the paper and the crumbs will fall together. Observe, you must not wipe above half a yard [about 45cm] at a stroke, and after doing all the upper part, go round again, beginning a little above where you left off. If you don't do it extremely lightly, you will make the dirt adhere to the paper.*

If you do not happen to possess a bellows, check to see if there is a 'blow' rather than a 'suck' setting on your vacuum cleaner, or enlist some children to make a game of blowing on the wallpaper. Or simply use a long-handled duster.

Living areas

Conduct a more thorough version of the weekly routine. Make a point of dusting items that are sometimes neglected – television, light fittings, etc. Dust and if necessary wash all ornaments. (Before doing this, Her Ladyship always thinks carefully about whether or not to bother. Most ornaments, she believes, are merely dust magnets that would look better on the shelves of a charity shop than on her own windowsills. It is for the benefit of those who abhor dusting that the concept of minimalism was invented.)

Wash or dry-clean cushion covers, throws or other removable upholstery. Consider inviting in a professional to clean upholstery and carpets.

Go through collections of DVDs and CDs and dispose of any that have not been watched or listened to since the last spring-clean. Anything that children have grown out of but that has sentimental value or may be of interest to as yet unborn grandchildren should go in the attic. (Her Ladyship actually believes it should go to the charity shop, but realises that some might find this attitude harsh.) Consider overflowing bookshelves and be realistic about books to which you are never going to refer again. Add them to the charity shop's heap.

Dining area

The same principles apply here. This is the time to do the waxing and polishing described on page 25; to decide whether a certain table cloth or set of napkins has become too scruffy to be used again (in which case it might be worth cutting them up to turn into cleaning rags); and to polish any silver that has been neglected since the last dinner party.

CLEANING THE CHANDELIER

Not every modern household faces this problem. Even Her Ladyship no longer owns a chandelier. However, if you are fortunate enough to have one, the joy of it is that the crystal sparkles when the sunlight strikes it, rather than shaming you by showing up every streak and speck of dust.

In former times, a housemaid would remove each droplet of a chandelier, wash it, rinse it and pat it dry. By all means do this if you are happy standing on a ladder balancing two separate buckets of water and several lint-free cloths for drying. If not, use a widely available spray-on 'chandelier and crystal cleaner'. Cover the floor below with newspaper (or, as one enterprising expert suggests, hang an old umbrella under the chandelier) and spray thoroughly, avoiding any electrical parts. Both dirt and excess spray will drop on to the newspaper or umbrella and the droplets will dry to a sparkling finish without your going to the trouble of polishing them.

Bedrooms

As before, dust and clean everywhere. Move furniture; vacuum and clean walls behind it.

Wash or dry-clean duvets, pillows, mattress covers and anything else that is not changed on a weekly or fortnightly basis. Carry out any of the tasks listed under *The Bedroom* (page 33) that have been neglected since the last spring-clean.

Sort through your wardrobe and try to make other adults in your household do the same. The rule of thumb is that anything that has not been worn for two years is not going to be worn again and should be disposed of. The only exceptions are ball gowns or elegant wedding outfits, which may be kept providing you have a reasonable expectation of being invited to a suitable occasion in the near future. Clear children's wardrobes and toy cupboards of anything that is no longer needed and store the surplus in the attic or give it to smaller children.

Kitchen

If you haven't done this recently, clean the oven and fridge as described on pages 38–41. Unplug the fridge, pull it gently away from the wall and clean the floor underneath. Vacuum or brush down the working parts at the back. Do the same with the washing machine and dishwasher, being careful not to disturb the plumbing arrangements.

Cupboard by cupboard, remove all crockery, glassware, cookware, etc. and wash the shelves and sides of the cupboards. Wash (or consider giving to a charity shop) crockery that has gathered dust because it has not been used since last spring. Empty and clean the cupboard under the sink and the drawers that hold cutlery, tea towels and other paraphernalia. Ruthlessly throw away any bowls with missing lids, lids with missing bowls and the 15-year-old tin of Brasso with a half-centimetre of cleaner encrusted on the bottom. Add the pineapple slicer that was a Christmas present three years ago and has never been used to the by now impressive collection of things to be given to charity.

Perform the same cleaning and throwing-out exercise with the larder and food cupboards. Her Ladyship has a casual attitude to the 'best before' dates of such things as herbs, spices and the dry ingredients for baking, but feels that this is nevertheless the time to dispose of herbs that no longer have any aroma at all and desiccated coconut of the same vintage as the tin of Brasso.

When restoring things to cupboards, do it tidily and systematically. Have a shelf for savoury foods and another for sweet ones. Use drawer dividers to separate cooking utensils that are used frequently – wooden spoons, potato peelers, spatulas – from the fondue forks, pâté knives and biscuit cutters. And, by the way – fondue forks? Pâté knives? Unless you are a regular thrower of '70s retro parties, these no longer justify house room.

Clean tiles behind the sink and cooker thoroughly. If they have a shiny surface and aren't, for example, inlaid with gold or platinum, apply a thin layer of car wax to the clean tiles. This will make day-to-day wiping of spills easier.

A TIP ABOUT THROWING THINGS AWAY
This applies not just to the kitchen but to any part of the house where clearing out (as opposed to tidying up) is being done. Ask yourself, 'Would I take this with me if I moved house? Would I pay someone else to pack it up for me?' If the answer is no, out it goes.

Bathroom

Again, perform a more thorough version of the weekly routine. Pay particular attention to soap scum or limescale that may have built up while no one was looking. Polish handles and taps.

Clean out the bathroom cabinet. As in the kitchen, throw away the last half-centimetre of hand cream in a bottle that has been there for years. Dispose of out-of-date medicines responsibly, but do please dispose of them.

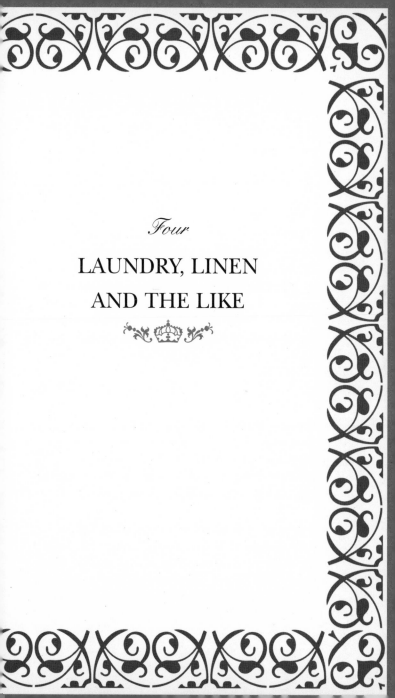

Four

LAUNDRY, LINEN
AND THE LIKE

In olden days it was not thought derogatory to the dignity of mistress or daughters of the house to assist with the home washing, and now, in households where only one or two servants are kept, it is most essential that the mistress should consider whether they have really time to do the washing properly if no aid is given, also if they really understand how it should be done, for both knowledge and patience are absolutely essential to make washing at home a satisfactory process.

Mrs Beeton's Cookery Book, 1911 edition

At the time those words were written, there was a continuing debate about whether the family washing should be done at home or sent out to a laundress. Mrs Beeton, rather controversially, advocated 'home washing', not only to save on laundry bills but more importantly to reduce wear and tear on clothes:

> *Where there are children…it is easily proved that the little garments carefully washed at home will last twice the time that they would if sent to a laundry, where certainly in nine cases out of ten, chemicals are used to make the linen a good colour and save labour at the expense of the clothing. Few ordinary laundresses wash flannels as they should be washed, so that when clean and dry they retain their original softness and clearness.*

Today washing machines take the place of the laundress and care instructions on garments take the guesswork out of laundry. But Mrs Beeton's advice about children's clothes and other 'delicates' remains valid. Washing by hand, using detergents designed for the purpose, in water of the recommended temperature, helps to prevent woollens from shrinking and colours from running. Detergents intending for hand-washing may also be used in twin tubs. They should not be used in front-loading machines: their extra frothiness is liable to spill out over the floor, as Her Ladyship learned to her cost in a moment of carelessness.

Soap-based detergents are more environmentally friendly than chemical ones, but soap itself is a less effective cleaning agent than modern detergents. Rather than go into the chemistry of this, Her Ladyship refers her readers to the soapy scum that can accumulate on shower screens and curtains. This is the result of soap reacting with water and, in the context of laundry, can leave clothes greyer and less bright than they should be. The best solution, in eco-terms, is a biodegradable detergent.

Most automatic washing machines rinse thoroughly (but see the note about towels on page 70). When washing by hand, however, rinsing properly is up to you. Inadequate rinsing leaves fabrics matted and harsh-feeling, and the residue of detergent may irritate the skin. Some washing machines have programmes that will rinse even delicate fabrics. Otherwise, rinse in lukewarm water under a running tap until the water runs away completely clear. This can be a tedious process, but it is in the long-term interests of your clothes. When hand-washing, remember that these garments are called delicate for a reason: do not rub vigorously, wring or twist. To remove excess water before hanging a wool or silk garment out to dry, roll it in a colourfast towel and squeeze gently.

If a care label recommends that a garment be dried flat, Her Ladyship begs her readers to obey. Wool in particular will quickly lose its shape if it is hung over a washing line or clothes dryer and left to drip: the water seeps to the bottom of the garment and stretches it in an uneven and unsightly way.

Towel care

'Buy the best you can afford' is Her Ladyship's advice here as with most things. For towels, pure cotton is softer, longer-lasting and more absorbent than most cotton mixes.

Towels will not remain soft if the slightest residue of soap remains in them after washing. Reducing the amount of washing powder by half will go a long way towards avoiding this; those with scant regard for their electricity bills and the environment may also choose to wash towels a second time with no washing powder at all.

An alternative is to use vinegar, adding a capful either to a basin of water as a 'pre-soak' or to the washing machine's rinse compartment. Her Ladyship does not recommend fabric conditioner for towels, as it coats them and makes them less absorbent. If you live in a hard-water area, adding water softener (according to the washing-machine makers' instructions) is, however, a good idea.

Towels will not remain soft if the slightest residue of soap remains in them after washing.

Whatever washing and rinsing approach you use, remove towels from the washing machine and fluff them up before drying, then fluff them up again after drying and before folding. Even if you prefer to dry towels on a washing line, giving them a few minutes' spin in the dryer before hanging them out in the garden improves softness.

A TIP FOR FOLDING TOWELS

Instead of folding a towel in half, spread it out on a flat surface and fold a third of it in towards the centre, then fold the opposite third over the top of that. The result will be a long thin strip. Turn it through 90 degrees and repeat the process with the other dimension. This will produce a parcel nine layers thick and approximately square.

Towels of any size from hand towels to bath sheets will stack better, wobble less and, if they are positioned fold-side outwards, look tidier when stored in this way.

A TIP TO SPEED UP DRYING

The British climate means that anyone who doesn't choose to dry everything by machine must sometimes hang laundry over a clothes horse or 'maiden' indoors. If you do your washing in the evening and hang it indoors overnight, take a moment next morning to turn it over, so that the side that was facing down (and is probably still damp) is now facing up and exposed to the air. Almost everything will dry more quickly and evenly this way.

Ironing

One of the novice housekeeper's most frequent questions is, 'What should I iron?' Her Ladyship's short answer is 'Anything that will look worse if you don't.' Almost all outer wear – blouses, skirts, dresses, jumpers, trousers – looks better when it is ironed, though this is less true of synthetic fabrics than it is of cotton, linen or wool.

Good-quality bedding cries out to be immaculately smooth. Those who dislike ironing may purchase polyester-cotton, which emerges from the dryer or washing line in an acceptable condition. They will, however, be denying themselves the considerable sensual pleasure that pure cotton and linen provide (see *Bed linen*, page 78). The brushed polycotton of Her Ladyship's youth should be avoided by anyone whose idea of sensual pleasure does not include a mild electric shock on retiring.

To iron fitted sheets, begin with the edges, fitting one corner round the pointed end of the ironing board. Iron the 'exposed' area, then move the sheet round and iron again until all the perimeter has been done. Fold the sheet into quarters lengthways (do this with a flat sheet too), so that most of the width will fit on the ironing board. Iron the uppermost surface, then turn it over and iron the other side. Invert the fold so that the unironed surfaces are now exposed and repeat the process. Note that this works only if the original folding is done neatly (see box opposite) – ironing will reinforce any creases left in by slipshod folding. The true ironaholic will carefully press each of the longitudinal folds in the sheet, so that when it is opened on the bed neatly spaced parallel creases will be revealed.

On the other hand, only the genuinely crease-phobic iron towels, dusters, underwear, socks and tracksuits.

Once the ironing is finished, don't put it away immediately – it will become creased again. Leave clothes hanging outside the wardrobe for at least half an hour or even overnight to ensure that they keep their immaculate look.

TIP FOR FOLDING A FITTED SHEET

This is much easier if you have two pairs of hands available; if not, home-making guru Martha Stewart gives the following advice. If you are left-handed, reverse the instructions for right and left:

Hold the sheet inside out and place one hand in each of the two corners of one of the shorter edges. Bring your right hand to your left and fold the corner in your right hand over the one in your left. Reach down, pick up the corner that is hanging in front of you and fold it over the two corners in your left hand; the corner that's showing will be inside out. Bring the last corner up and fold it over the others with its right side showing. Lay the folded sheet on a flat surface and straighten it so that all the elasticated edges sit neatly on top of one another. Fold the two outside edges in so that the elastic is hidden. Fold the sheet into a rectangle, then continue folding until the rectangle is the size you want it to be.

TIPS FOR REDUCING IRONING

• Remove laundry from the washing machine as soon as the cycle is finished.

• Untangle individual items: it is extraordinary how intimately the legs of two pairs of trousers can intertwine in the washing machine. Smooth them out before putting them in the dryer. Again, remove laundry from the dryer as soon as the cycle is finished. Smooth it and fold it neatly. Those who are happy to present a casual appearance will then find that jeans and garments made of stretch fabrics can be worn without ironing.

• If you are drying laundry on a line, take the trouble to hang it neatly. Hang all 'separates' from the waistband, so that trousers hang the right way up and shirts upside down. This means you can put the pegs on inconspicuous parts of the garments: peg marks on shoulders are particularly unsightly and pull clothes out of shape.

• Ease delicate items such as knitwear back into shape while they are still damp and dry them flat on a colourfast towel.

• Kill two birds with one stone. Use a damp sheet as a second cover for your ironing board. Fold the sheet neatly, drape it over the board and iron smaller items on top of it. When the exposed part of the sheet is smooth, edge it up over the board to expose another bit. By the time you have finished ironing your clothes, you will have ironed a sheet or two as well.

The wardrobe

One of the most important aspects of storing clothes is to give them breathing space. If you squash them too close together you will have to iron them all over again before you can wear them; they will also be more prone to damp, moths and all the other horrors of neglected clothes – anyone who has teenage sons who leave sportswear lying in a heap on the floor will understand why Her Ladyship would prefer not to go into further details.

In an ideal world, a wardrobe should not be positioned against an outside wall, which may be prone not only to damp but to harmful extremes of temperature. With a fitted wardrobe you have no choice, which makes the advice about damp and breathing space given throughout this chapter all the more important.

In an ideal world, a wardrobe should not be positioned against an outside wall.

Hanging and hangers

Hanging woollen garments will cause them to lose their shape: it's much better to fold them and keep them on shelves or in drawers with plenty of space. Never cram more items into a drawer that it will comfortably hold.

Most other clothing – cotton, linen, dresses, skirts, shirts, trousers – can be hung on hangers in the wardrobe.

Remove garments that have been dry-cleaned from their packaging (particularly if it is plastic) before putting them away. Left for any length of time, a plastic cover will make fabric damp and more liable to mould; perversely, it will also dry out leather or suede.

Wooden hangers are preferable to wire, which can bend clothing out of shape and are easily bent themselves. Padded hangers are best for delicate fabrics. Her Ladyship has an innate aversion to plastic in most of its forms, and most plastic hangers are too light to be useful for any but the flimsiest garments.

Trousers should always be hung with belt removed, pockets emptied and fastenings fastened. Hold them by the bottoms of the legs, line up the side seams on each leg, then line the left leg up with the right. Smooth away any obvious wrinkles. Arrange over the cross-bar of the hanger so that the legs hang slightly lower than the waist – the waistband and seat of the trousers are heavier than the legs, so this distributes the weight more evenly than if the fold comes halfway down.

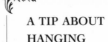

A TIP ABOUT HANGING
After taking off a suit that you plan to wear again before having it cleaned, hang it outside the wardrobe – on the door handle, perhaps, or from the top of a door – for an hour or so to give it breathing (and wrinkle-losing) space.

Storing clothes for the seasons

If your wardrobe (that is, the number of garments you possess) is too large for your wardrobe (the piece of furniture), then clothes that are 'out of season' should be carefully stored away.

There are two important considerations to the storing of clothes. One, they should be clean. Two, they should be stored in suitable containers that allow them room to breathe and do not attract insects. A perfectly clean suitcase lined with acid-free paper is ideal; brand-new cardboard boxes, similarly lined, are also suitable. Wrap clothing in acid-free paper or natural fabric – not plastic, which promotes mould. Place lightweight items on top of heavier ones rather than the other way around (this is, once again, to do with breathing space: no one wants their precious silks to suffocate). Insert a wood block or bag of herbs (see box opposite) between every few layers of garments to deter moths. Store somewhere dark, dry and away from direct heat.

A TIP FOR DRAWERS AND WARDROBES

Keep these smelling fresh with bags of herbs or small blocks of sandalwood or cedar, all of which have the added advantage of repelling moths. There is no need to splash out on bags of ready-made pot-pourri: many garden herbs and kitchen spices serve the same purpose. Her Ladyship recommends cinnamon sticks, cloves, rosemary, mint, thyme or dried lemon peel as well as the more familiar dried lavender. Suitable bags can be made from any leftover cotton fabric or from muslin, which you will find in the jam-making section of kitchen shops.

Cedar and sandalwood need to be rough if they are to be effective, so sand them lightly before use and again after six months. Be warned, however, that neither herb sachets nor wooden blocks remain effective for ever. Replace them as soon as they begin to lose their fragrance, at least once a year.

An alternative to all this is to use a bar of scented soap. In addition to the protection that this will give your clothes, exposure to air dries the soap, so when you remove it from your lingerie drawer and use it in the bathroom it will last longer.

If by any chance you possess old-fashioned mothballs, dispose of them instantly and with the utmost care. Do not leave them anywhere near children or pets and do not flush them down the lavatory. The naphthalene-based ones that our great-grandparents used are now known to be both toxic and carcinogenic; mid-twentieth-century versions contained paradichlorobenzene, which is still used to clean public lavatories and is not something Her Ladyship would choose to put anywhere near her own clothes.

Bed linen

Although what we know as bed linen and table linen were indeed originally made of linen, these are now generic terms that can cover articles made of cotton or other materials too. Do not, dear Reader, be frightened into thinking that all your bedding must be of linen: if you do, no matter how luxurious is it, you will endure long wakeful nights fretting about the ironing.

How much bed linen you need depends entirely on how many beds you have and how often they are used. For a bed that is in constant use, Her Ladyship recommends three sets of sheets, pillow cases and duvet covers: one on the bed, one in the wash and a spare, in case for some reason the laundry is not done that week

Her Ladyship recommends three sets of sheets, pillow cases and duvet covers: one on the bed, one in the wash and a spare.

(even Her Ladyship's grandmother, running a large household along rigorously Victorian lines, allowed her housekeeper occasional time off for unforeseen eventualities). For spare-room bedding, two sets are sufficient. Egyptian cotton is cool and pleasurable for mild weather; today's centrally heated homes make it unnecessary to change to brushed cotton for winter, but this still gives a cosy feeling on cold nights.

Assuming duvets are the chosen bed covering, there should be at least one for every bed and sufficient spares to see the household through the twice-yearly dry-cleaning period (see page 82) or an unexpected bout of visitors. The warmth and weight of a duvet is measured by the 'tog' system: as a rough guide, 4.5 tog is generally recommended for summer use, 9–11 for spring and autumn, up to 13.5 for winter. This guide must, of course, be adapted to suit individual attitudes to being warm or cool in bed. One practical approach is to buy a lightweight and a medium-weight duvet which may be used individually during the appropriate seasons but are designed to be joined together to make a warm winter covering.

Visually speaking, a duvet is all the covering a bed requires: there is no need for a bedspread to make it look 'finished'. Some people, however, like to fold an embroidered throw across the foot of the bed: this is decorative during the day; weighs the duvet down just a little when the bed is in use, making it less likely to fall off in the night; and can be pulled up to form an extra layer if it turns cold in the small hours.

If you prefer blankets to duvets – and many people do, because they like to feel 'tucked in' at night – wool is the best option. In addition to being warm, it is hypoallergenic and more fire-retardant that most manmade alternatives. The number of blankets required again depends on your attitude to warmth, but three per bed (two in use plus a spare) is a sensible functioning minimum. Eiderdowns and bedspreads are a matter of taste, but are desirable on a blanket-covered bed: unlike duvets, blankets alone do not make a bed look 'made'.

In Her Ladyship's youth, every pillow had two cases: the plain, close-fitting 'housewife' type which protected the pillow but was still easy to remove when it needed to be washed; and the looser Oxford style which had a stitched border, matched the sheets and looked elegant. Nowadays, housewife pillowcases are sold in many colours and in pleasing fabrics such as Egyptian cotton. Where there are two pillows (per person) on a bed, the housewife may be used for the bottom one and the Oxford for the top. Many people now dispense with the perceived extravagance of two cases per pillow, but Her Ladyship has a nostalgic fondness for it.

There has lately been much anxious public discussion over how often sheets should be changed. Her Ladyship was brought up on 'once a week, without fail'; she realises that there are those who consider that an old-fashioned view, though it is still strongly held by most of her own acquaintance. Those who think changing the sheets every week is an intolerable burden should be grateful that they don't live in Victorian times, when stripping and airing every bed and beating and turning every mattress every day was commonplace in any respectable household. Whatever your views on your own bedding, guests – even if they are staying only one night and unless they are teenagers who bring their own sleeping bags and sleep on the floor – should always be accorded the courtesy of clean bedding.

In Her Ladyship's youth, before duvets were commonplace in Britain, it was the custom in some households to change the bottom sheet every week, replacing it with the top (less dirty) one and putting a clean sheet on the top. She would suggest – with perhaps just a touch of hauteur – that this habit belongs to the period of post-war austerity in which turning threadbare sheets 'sides to middle' and having a bath only once a week were also common practice. However, if, like Her Ladyship, you find changing the duvet cover a constant battle (see page 82), make the bed with a top sheet between the duvet and the sleeping person. You can then get away with changing the duvet cover only once a fortnight, as long as you change the sheets every week. The topmost pillowcase should be changed once a week; the housewife (either on a second pillow or the second case on the top pillow) can last a fortnight.

Although it is no longer the chore it once was, airing the bed is still a healthy thing to do. In the interests once again of killing two birds with one stone, Her Ladyship offers this time-saving advice: open the bedroom windows first thing in the morning, if they are not open already, and pull all the bedcovers back before going to have a shower. The bed will have aired itself by the time you return.

Mattress covers

Her Ladyship's ancestors – indeed, most people's ancestors, though many would disdain to admit it – slept on a horsehair mattress, which was covered by a blanket and then by a heavy cotton undersheet. A more delicate cotton or linen sheet on top of that protected the sleeper from any lingering odour or texture of horse. Today's fabrics are more hygienic, but a good washable padded cotton mattress cover is nevertheless essential to protect your mattress from dust mites and various types of spillage or leakage, mentionable or otherwise. The key word here is, of course, washable, as the cover can then be removed regularly (about once a month) and laundered.

Sheepskin mattress covers are appreciably more expensive than cotton, but their admirers claim that they promote good sleep and are the ultimate in comfort, particularly for those suffering from back ache, arthritis, rheumatism or – and Her Ladyship can hardly bear to ask her secretary to type this – bed sores. They tend to be 'dry-clean only', but you may feel that this is a small price to pay for such an impressive list of benefits.

Changing the duvet cover

Her Ladyship has been performing this task once a week for a number of decades and still finds it a struggle. However, in theory the technique is as follows:

• **Lay the duvet flat on the bed** – or at least sufficiently flat that two corners of the short side are readily accessible. (Her Ladyship is aware that some duvets and their covers are square and thus have no short side; she would ask her readers to use their common sense in such a case.)

• **Turn the duvet cover inside out** and slide your arms inside it to grasp the two far corners. Holding fast to those corners, take hold of the two readily accessible corners of the duvet.

• **Still holding all four corners** (two of the cover, two of the duvet itself) firmly, shake and slide the cover down the duvet. If necessary, lay the duvet on the bed and tidy the rest of the cover – the corners of the duvet that are inside the cover should by this time have realised who is boss and be prepared to stay where they belong.

• **Fasten the open side** and place it at the foot of the bed.

Cleaning duvets and pillows

These should be washed or dry-cleaned, depending on what the care label advises, at least once every six months. Washing a duvet requires either an industrial-sized machine (available at many launderettes) or a bath tub. If you use the latter, you may prefer to leave the duvet to soak in soapy water or get into the bath and trample on it rather than risk damaging your back by washing in a more conventional manner. Rinse and dry thoroughly. Drying a duvet naturally – out of doors if possible, dripping over the bath if not – will probably take two days.

If blankets rather than a duvet are the bedding of choice, have them dry-cleaned once a month or so.

The linen cupboard

A linen cupboard should have slatted shelves to allow the materials to breathe; traditionally these are made of cedar, to guard against moth attack. Nowadays many linen cupboards double as airing cupboards, being a number of slatted shelves placed above the hot-water tank. However well lagged that tank may be, a little warmth will always escape and help to keep the linen in the cupboard fresh and dry.

Rarely used items such as spare blankets should be stored on the top shelf, leaving the easily accessible shelves for the linen that is needed most frequently.

Her Ladyship recommends dividing sheets and duvet covers according to size, so that all the single items are together, as are all the doubles and all the queens or kings. For maximum efficiency, mark each item with laundry marker to indicate its size: a simple S, D, Q or K will suffice. If you fold and store your linen with the mark facing outwards, you'll be able to identify an individual item even if the piles become confused. A separate pile for pillowcases makes these easy to find should a careless guest ever spill a cup of tea over the one in use.

In Victorian times, it was part of a housekeeper's job to organise the linen so that it was used in strict rotation; each item thus received the same amount of wear. Her Ladyship believes there is a great deal of common sense in this approach. In today's smaller households the desired result can be achieved simply by placing a newly laundered item on the top of its pile and using the item from the bottom. Make sure that taking out the bottom item doesn't upset the pile or you will make a mockery of the time-honoured system you are trying to replicate.

Five

DINNER AND SUPPER
PARTIES

Hospitality is a most excellent virtue; but care must be taken that the love of company, for its own sake, does not become a prevailing passion, for then the habit is no longer hospitality, but dissipation… as Washington Irving well says, 'There is an emanation from the heart in genuine hospitality, which cannot be described, but is immediately felt, and puts the stranger at once at his ease.'

Isabella Beeton, *Book of Household Management*, 1861

Putting guests at their ease is indeed a key part of any form of entertaining, but it cannot be achieved if the host and hostess do not give the appearance of being relaxed too. Giving the impression (which may not be entirely false) of enjoying your own parties necessitates putting effort into planning and preparation. That is why much of this chapter is concerned with what to do before your guests arrive. A solo host/ess in particular does not want to run the risk of a meal being ruined by a guest ringing the doorbell at a crucial moment. Nor do you want to be obliged to ignore your guests and miss out on their conversation while putting the finishing touches to a complicated meal.

Issuing invitations

The most important aspect of an invitation is that it should tell the recipients what to expect. 'Canapés 6–8.30 p.m.' on a printed card *should* prevent anyone from expecting a four-course dinner and staying till midnight. For a later gathering, 'Carriages at 1 a.m.' was the form of words used when a carriage was the standard means of transport for anybody you were likely to consider inviting to a party. Nowadays it would be viewed as either stiffly formal or endearingly tongue-in-cheek. Use it, therefore, only if it is obvious which of those options you intend.

Even when invitations are issued verbally or by email, 'Come for dinner' means something different from 'Come for supper'. The former suggests a degree of formality; the latter could be shepherd's pie with the children round the kitchen table.

An important note for guests: if in any doubt about what the invitation means – whether in terms of what is being offered, dress code or other guests – ask. Perhaps the only thing worse than wearing unkempt jeans to a formal dinner is turning up in a glamorous gown to a casual supper.

Perhaps the only thing worse than wearing unkempt jeans to a formal dinner is turning up in a glamorous gown to a casual supper.

And be aware of different nationalities' attitudes to mealtimes: Her Ladyship was once almost caught unawares by an invitation to 'come over' from an American friend. The time specified was 7 p.m., and it was only because she asked that Her Ladyship realised she was expected to have had her evening meal before she arrived.

If asking people casually for 'a drink', try tactfully to convey that neither dinner nor supper is included in the invitation. 'We need to be free to put the kids to bed by half-past seven, so why don't you come at six?' requires the existence of children too small to put themselves to bed, but is an approach that may be taken if such children exist. '…To help them with their homework' is a useful alternative with older children. But in the absence of offspring of any age, 'Why don't you pop in for an hour after work?' should serve the purpose. 'We have to go out at eight', though commendably unambiguous, is perhaps a little rude.

Occasionally guests, particularly those who are keen to share every detail of a recent heartbreak, fail to take this hint. In these circumstances, the caring hostess will have prepared a simple supper which can be offered if the guest shows no signs of departing and she herself is hungry. The tone in which 'I can offer you a bit of quiche' is said should indicate to all but the most insensitive whether the expected answer is 'Thank you, that would be lovely' or 'No, I really must be going.' If the worst comes to the worst and the children really do need to be put to bed, rising to your feet and saying, firmly but graciously, 'I'm going to have to throw you out' should finally put the message across.

Planning the meal

Assuming that guests *have* been invited for a meal, the difference
between supper and dinner is important. For a midweek after-
work supper, no one expects the culinary boat to be pushed out.
Even if you feel obliged to offer three courses, a homemade main
course, preceded by a few olives or char-grilled artichokes from
the local delicatessen or supermarket's deli counter and followed
by a shop-bought dessert, furbished with some fresh seasonal
berries if the shop hasn't done that already, is all that's required.

If more time is available for preparation and you choose to
go to more trouble – in other words, if you are offering dinner
rather than supper – the following may be a useful checklist of
things to consider:

• **Ease of preparation.** If you are serving a three-course meal, it is
only sensible to have at least one course fully prepared in advance.
A cold starter that can be arranged earlier in the day on individual
plates and moved from fridge to table perhaps 15 minutes before
the guests arrive is ideal in any but the coldest weather; a soup that
needs only to be reheated five minutes before serving is an easy
winter alternative. Cold puddings that require only a little last-
minute decoration are also a boon.

• **Probability of success.** Only the most dauntless cook tries out a
complicated new recipe on an important occasion. Close friends
and family are generally happy to be experimented on; if your
guests include a client or a demanding elderly relative, make
something you have made before and about which you feel
confident.

• **Balance.** A balanced meal rings the changes: a spicy starter
should be followed by a less fiery main course; a main course of
lamb tagine with apricots rules out a fruity pudding, while a rich

and creamy casserole might be followed by a citrus tart or fruit
salad rather than cheesecake or chocolate mousse.

• **Visual appeal.** In addition to a mix of tastes, the food should
have a mix of colours and textures. A dish that is predominantly
brown or white can be much enlivened by a sprinkling of herbs
or a serving of carrots. Garnishes do not have to consist of a pallid
lettuce leaf and a slice of cucumber – consider instead the visual
possibilities of slices of orange or kiwi fruit, a few halved
strawberries or a handful of pomegranate seeds. Those who feel
that fruit does not 'go' with meat or fish may admire the effect
without feeling obliged to eat it. Her Ladyship, mindful of those
self-styled experts who drone on about 'your five a day', always eats
a salad garnish, but this is a matter of personal preference: there is
no breach of etiquette in leaving it.

• **Guests' dietary requirements.** A thoughtful hostess will always
ascertain if any of her guests follows a special diet for religious,
cultural or medical reasons, or if they have any allergies or
particular dislikes. Do not, however, attempt the impossible: while
it is courteous and not difficult to provide a vegetarian option or
a lactose-free meal, no non-Jew can cater satisfactorily to the needs
of someone who keeps strict Kosher. Better to entertain such a
guest in a suitable restaurant, or to issue an invitation where the
entertainment is not centred round food.

However informal the meal, unless the invitation has specifically
included the words 'pot luck' or 'leftovers', there should always
be plenty of food. No guest at the most impromptu supper party
should feel obliged to count the number of potatoes in a serving
dish and divide that by the number of guests to ensure that he
does not take more than his share. If for whatever reason portion

control is an issue, take the 'dish everything up in the kitchen' approach described on page 105. But Her Ladyship is firmly of the opinion that portion control should *not* be an issue for a dinner with friends, unless it be for the good of the health of one of them.

Cheese before pudding?

This is the French way and the rationale is that it is better to end the meal with something sweet: the taste buds are satisfied. The English argument for serving pudding first is that cheese in general and Stilton in particular go so well with port, which used often to be served at the end of a meal. A touch of sweetness could then be achieved by serving chocolates with the coffee.

Her Ladyship has no strong views on this matter and is inclined to advise her readers to follow their own preferences. Serving cheese and pudding simultaneously and allowing guests to make up their own minds neatly circumvents the problem. The one thing she would advocate, however, is that if you do opt to serve the two courses separately, make it clear that there is something to follow. She has more than once felt mildly embarrassed at having partaken liberally of a cheese course, only to discover that she was then expected to do justice to a lavish pudding.

TIPS FOR UNCONFIDENT COOKS

When planning a menu, avoid, at all costs, anything that is likely to go wrong at the last minute. Possible problem areas include:

• stirring cream (or crème fraîche or anything of that sort) into hot soup just before serving. If the soup is too hot, the cream will curdle.

• Homemade hollandaise or béarnaise sauce. These take time and patience and will curdle if you try to make them quickly. Supermarkets and delis sell perfectly acceptable versions to serve with asparagus (hollandaise) or steak (béarnaise). In Her Ladyship's view, it is hard enough to cook asparagus to the right consistency or steak to the desired level of rareness or doneness without adding the complication of a sensitive sauce.

• Anything that requires flambéeing. It's just too stressful.

• Anything – roasted peppers, for example – that goes under a very hot grill at the last minute. If your attention wanders, they will burn.

• Soufflés. These require precision timing and tend to sink if you open the oven door to check on them at the wrong moment.

Setting the table

Do this before guests arrive. The more formal the occasion, the more complex it will be and the more the details matter. Whether or not you use a table cloth and mats depends on the surface of the table: beautifully polished wood, rough-hewn 'farmhouse' style tables or elegant glass are meant to be displayed. Less perfect surfaces should be covered by linen – traditionally white double damask, but many less formal materials, shades and patterns are now widely used. If using a cloth, make sure that it is centred on the table, so that any ironed-in creases run in straight lines and the overhang is the same on both sides.

The purpose of mats is to prevent the table being scorched or stained. Some, usually made of fabric, are large enough to serve as the base for the place setting (that is, the cutlery sits on top of them); with smaller, harder mats, the cutlery goes outside. Make sure you put enough mats in the centre to accommodate all the hot serving dishes you intend to put on the table – and make sure also that there are enough serving spoons to go with them.

An alternative to mats is a baize 'undercloth', over which the linen cloth is placed. Mrs Beeton points out that this 'enables the table cloth to lie better, and it is more pleasant to the touch with some soft, thick substance beneath it'. Certainly you don't want to run the risk of your cloth slipping about on the table and upsetting gravy into a guest's lap.

Cutlery should be arranged so that what is to be used for the first course is on the outside, followed by that for the second course and so on, working inwards towards the plate. Spoons and knives are always to the right of the plate, forks to the left, with the cutting edges of knives pointing inwards. There is no need to make a concession to

Spoons and knives are always to the right of the plate, forks to the left, with the cutting edges of knives pointing inwards.

left-handers here: not all of them eat with their cutlery the 'wrong' way round and those who do are generally capable of making the switch themselves.

Thus, depending on what is being served at the meal, the arrangement of cutlery (reading from furthest to nearest the plate) might be:

• **Soup spoon** or small spoon for hors d'oeuvre on the right

• **Fish knife** on the right, fish fork on the left

• **Main course knife** on the right, fork on the left

• **Pudding spoon** on the right, pudding fork, if required, on the left.

If you are serving a starter that requires a knife and fork, these implements should be smaller than those used for the main course (a standard dinner service contains knives and forks of two sizes for this reason).

A note about fish knives

'Fish eaters' (the utensils, not the people) were invented in the nineteenth century and adopted by the up-and-coming middle classes, while being frowned upon by the higher echelons of society: in the 1880s, etiquette books still advocated eating fish either with two ordinary forks or with a fork and a piece of bread. This disapproval of the new implements lasted for generations: in 1954 John Betjeman published a poem called 'How to Get On in Society' in which fish knives were lampooned alongside frills around cutlets and log fires that could be turned on with the flick of a switch.

Times change, however. Nowadays many people find that they have inherited a previous generation's canteen of cutlery that includes fish knives and forks, and don't know whether to use them or not. In this instance, Her Ladyship would simply ask her readers if they find the implements attractive and comfortable to use. If so, use them. She does herself and doesn't care what anyone thinks.

A bread plate, with accompanying knife, should be placed to the left of this basic setting and will serve double duty if cheese is served later. A napkin, neatly folded, may be placed on the bread plate under the knife; alternatively, it may sit in the centre of the place setting, where the main plates will go. Linen – freshly ironed – is best for all but the most informal of occasions. However, there are exceptions to this rule: colourful gingham (which still needs ironing but need not aspire to the same level of perfection) sits well on rough-hewn tables in farmhouse-style kitchens. If the dining room has a strong colour theme, matching napkins – whether fabric or, at a pinch, good-quality paper – may produce a striking effect. As an extreme example, Her Ladyship has a friend who holds supper parties in her large kitchen, where the table-top is made from tiles depicting sprigs of olives. The local supermarket sells paper napkins of almost exactly the same pattern. This pleasing piece of happenstance saves that particular hostess much laundering and ironing – and rarely fails to amuse her guests. On the other hand, Her Ladyship acknowledges that many people will find it more convenient to invest in suitable napkins than to buy a new table to match those available in Sainsbury's.

Glasses sit to the top right of the place setting; that is, above the cutlery, with the nearest glass lined up with the pudding spoon. The convention is that shorter glasses are placed closer to the diner than taller ones, so if you are using both red and white wine glasses, put the white wine glass closest to the cutlery, the red wine glass immediately behind it and the water glass to the right of the white wine glass. Glasses for white wine are normally smaller than those for red, making it easier to reach over the smaller glass to the larger rather than vice versa; it also makes the table look neater. No place setting is complete without a glass for water: even the most hardened of non-drivers may like a refreshing sip of water occasionally.

A note about napkins

First of all, this is what they are called. Nancy Mitford and
others who defined the vocabulary of class distinction in
the 1950s would turn in their graves to hear anyone use the
word 'serviette' and this is a piece of snobbery that (unlike
the one attaching to fish knives, see page 95) seems to have
stood the test of time. Second, whatever form they take,
they must be clean – nothing is more offputting at the start
of a meal than the suggestion of someone else's spinach on
your napkin. And third, anything is better than nothing.
As an absolutely last resort, if you possess no linen napkins
and have forgotten to buy paper ones, supply your guests
with kitchen roll rather than leave them to dab a spot of
tomato sauce away with their sleeve.

A digression concerning wine

While on the subject of wine glasses, Her Ladyship would like to express a perhaps controversial opinion on the subject of which wine goes with which food. Yes, chefs and oenologists alike have spent many decades studying the compatibility of certain tastes and yes, for the most part, red wine does go better with red meat and white wine with fish. But that axiom takes no account of personal taste. James Bond, travelling on the Orient Express in *From Russia with Love*, may have identified a villain because he ordered Chianti with fish; Her Ladyship, quietly confident that none of her guests is going to turn out to be a counter-intelligence agent, would – with the utmost grace – permit them to drink what they like.

That said, many people prefer to start the evening with white wine and move on to red for the main course. Choose wines that you think will complement the food – there are wine books and newspaper columns galore to help you out. If guests bring wine, think of this as a present – you are under no obligation to open it then and there. On the other hand, if you know that your guest is knowledgeable about wine and she says, 'I'd love to try that if you don't mind', it would be churlish to refuse.

The other time to open the guest's offering is if it is cheap and unpleasant-looking and you know that that particular guest makes a habit of bringing cheap and unpleasant wine to parties. Her Ladyship has one friend who forced an offending guest to drink the rubbish he had brought by the simple expedient of offering no alternative, while surreptitiously topping up her own glass with a decent Burgundy in the kitchen.

There is nowadays no stigma whatsoever attached to wine that comes with a screw top. Many of the best wines from Australia and New Zealand, among others, are bottled this way. Although this removes some of the ritual of wine serving and in particular deprives you of the immensely enjoyable sound of a healthy cork

being popped, there remains the even more pleasurable glug-glug-glug of the wine being poured and the knowledge that what is in your glass is likely to be pleasurable too.

Once dinner is served, Her Ladyship – frequently entertaining on her own – chooses to leave wine bottles on the table and invite guests to help themselves. If there are two hosts and no more than six people, then each host serving his or her neighbours works well; more than that and it becomes awkward. If a guest at the far end of the table seems to be sitting with an empty glass, a specific invitation to 'top yourself up' normally results in bottles being passed around and everyone being kept happy.

Leaving the wine out of reach on the sideboard means that whoever has been delegated to serve it has to keep leaping up and down, interrupting his own meal while keeping a vigilant eye out for anyone whose glass needs replenishing. In Her Ladyship's view this is a task best left for those rare occasions when a butler is present, and not to be trusted to any hostess's husband (and he is all too common a breed) who is notorious for becoming engrossed in conversation and neglecting his duties as a host.

Ice buckets are too large and too prone to causing upsets to sit on the table. If white wine is likely to linger long enough to become warmer than you would like it to be, a wine cooler is a better option. This does not mean the kind that you keep in the freezer that can chill warm wine in minutes

If white wine is likely to linger long enough to become warmer than you would like it to be, a wine cooler is a better option.

(though these are invaluable in a white-wine emergency), but the 'double-walled' acrylic ones that keep chilled wine cool for an hour or two. These are perhaps too casual for formal dinner parties, but in those circumstances you may well stop serving white wine and move on to red before the temperature of the former becomes an issue. If not, an ice bucket on a conveniently placed side table is the answer.

TWO PREPARATORY NOTES

Make sure that the dishwasher is empty before guests arrive
and that the last lot of clean dishes has been put away. This
makes clearing up at the end of the evening much easier
(see page 112).

Also make sure that you have all the plates and serving
dishes you need in readiness. It is a shame to allow food to
spoil while you rummage in the cupboard for a suitable dish
in which to serve the beans. Put plates and serving dishes
for the main course (assuming it is hot) in a low oven or
warming drawer about half an hour before they are
needed: you want them to be gently warm rather than
scalding. Never bring saucepans to the table unless they
are Le Creuset or other oven-to-tableware designed
for the purpose.

Table decorations

Her Ladyship recommends not necessarily minimalism, but
certainly restraint in the matter of decorating the table.
Decorations should never take up so much space that there is
insufficient room for the food; nor should they obstruct anyone's
view of anyone else. The elaborate epergnes that adorned the
tables of Louis XIV and the Prince Regent were designed to show
off the owner's wealth (a piece of vulgarity of which Her Ladyship
is sure her readers would never be guilty); they also belong to an
era of strict etiquette when it was considered ill manners to speak
to someone sitting on the other side of the table.

With today's less formal attitudes, a few candles or tea lights
in an attractive holder add to the atmosphere, as long as it is dark

outside. They are faintly ridiculous at lunchtime or on a summer's evening when it is still broad daylight. Use only unscented candles, lest they compete with the aromas of the food. Make sure tall candles are steady in their holders and also that the flame will not be at anyone's eye level. Light them just before you are ready to eat and blow them out only when guests have gone or when you leave the table.

Flowers, once *de rigueur* as a centrepiece on any dinner table, are probably better placed on a side table – again, because of the issue of conflicting scents and also because a careless arm reaching for salt and pepper may upset them. If you do want flowers, make sure they are minimally scented and, as Mrs Beeton puts it, 'either high enough or low enough not to impede the view'. See page 31 for a few of Her Ladyship's thoughts on flower arranging.

When guests arrive

It is a basic courtesy to give guests somewhere to hang their coats and to leave bags, umbrellas and other paraphernalia. If your own coats take up all the available space, move them to a cupboard in the spare room or heap them on a bed somewhere out of sight. Alternatively, ask guests to leave their things in a bedroom whose bed and floor are clear and clean enough not to cause embarrassment to the hostess or disgust to the visitor.

While it is polite to greet guests with such remarks as 'How lovely to see you' or 'You found it all right then?', you should offer them a drink promptly. However engaging the conversation, one's visitors have come in the expectation of receiving hospitality and there is nothing like not being offered a drink to make one realise one is gasping for one. If drinks are accompanied by 'nibbles', these should be laid out before the guests arrive and handed round with the first drink. Thereafter, you can simply invite people to 'help themselves'.

In a gathering of fewer than about ten people, make sure that everyone is introduced to everyone else. With larger numbers this becomes cumbersome, but even then each new arrival must be introduced to someone or brought to the attention of someone they already know so that they are not left alone while you fetch them a

In a gathering of fewer than about ten people, make sure that everyone is introduced to everyone else.

drink. An introduction requires more than a mere exchange of names: snippets of information such as 'Marie and I used to work together' or 'David belongs to the same tennis club as I do' prevent either Marie or David having to begin the conversation with a laboured 'So how do you know Her Ladyship?'

Aim to serve the first course of a meal about 30–45 minutes after the time for which people have been invited. This allows latecomers to relax and have a drink without feeling rushed, but also reduces the risk of the punctual being ready for a third drink before they have anything to eat.

A TIP FOR SOLO HOSTS

If you are entertaining more than about four people, invite one of them to come early and act as bartender for the first twenty minutes. If you are torn between tending the kitchen, answering the doorbell and pouring wine, the wine is likely to be neglected (which is a social *faux pas*, but preferable to the food being ruined). Having another person acting as co-host at this moment saves a lot of harassment. If appropriate, be sure to choose someone who can open a champagne bottle efficiently and is familiar with your style of corkscrew.

Seating plans

Her Ladyship mentally prepares a seating plan whenever she
invites more than two or three people to a meal. Other hostesses
favour a more relaxed, 'sit where you like' approach, though most
will add, 'I like to sit...', indicating the seat nearest the kitchen or
most convenient for whatever she needs to do. Even having been
told to sit where he likes, no guest should ever sit without
establishing that this is not the hostess's preferred position.

For formal or large gatherings, it is sensible to label each
place with the person's name on a small card. Position it 'top
centre' of the individual setting. For smaller parties, however,
it is enough for the hostess to point each guest to his or her
allocated position.

The traditional rules are to alternate the sexes and to
separate partners, but this may not always be possible and should
never be enforced so rigidly as to make anyone uncomfortable.
Her Ladyship has many single female friends who make congenial
dinner guests (and one or two male ones too) and frankly
doesn't give a damn about balancing the numbers of the genders.
Rather, she suggests that you consider how well the guests know
each other and how people who don't know each other are likely
to get on. Don't seat people of fiercely opposing political or
religious views together unless you are quite certain that everyone
at the table – and not just the two participants – will enjoy the
ensuing argument.

In a group where one person is likely to feel left out or shy
– an old friend's new partner, for instance – place this guest,
regardless of gender, next to the hostess or host. You can then
ensure that he is well looked after and included in the
conversation, while at the same time getting to know him better.

Give thought, also, to the size, age and mobility of guests.
Anyone who is heavily pregnant or for any other reason likely to
need frequent access to the loo should be placed in the most

convenient position for surreptitious leaving of the room. Only the young and slim should be invited to 'clamber round the back' if one side of the table is less accessible than the other.

Serving

On formal occasions, food is always served from the diner's left and drink from the right. The latter is only prudent, as glasses are placed on the right of the place setting and serving food from the left minimises the risk of stretching, spilling and knocking over. But insisting on serving food from the left assumes the presence of a butler or footman, which is no longer a feature of the home of most of Her Ladyship's acquaintance.

There used also to be an etiquette concerning the serving of vegetables – the most seasonal was served first, presumably to emphasise its freshness; potatoes were served last, whatever the season. In the modern household, Her Ladyship feels, this is an unnecessary piece of protocol. There is nothing wrong with placing vegetables in warmed serving dishes (see page 101) on the table and asking guests to help themselves. If the main dish is in casserole form, the hostess can put it in front of her place and serve it in full view of the guests.

If the main dish is in casserole form, the hostess can put it in front of her place and serve it in full view of the guests.

She may choose to do the same with something like steak or whole trout, when everyone is served with a single item. With a joint, unless you are an adept carver, carry out this delicate operation in the privacy of the kitchen and bring in the carved meat on a platter.

Some hostesses serve everything, including vegetables, in the kitchen, and hand each guest a full plate on which the food is elegantly arranged. The only disadvantage of this is that anyone with a small appetite has to draw attention to herself in order to be served less generously; it is perfectly acceptable if you are confident that all your guests are hearty eaters.

If you, as hostess, are doing the dishing up, try either to serve out everything or to leave enough to be able to offer second helpings. If people are enthusiastic enough about the food to come back for more, you don't want six guests wondering how to divide three potatoes and a spoonful of broccoli between them.

Etiquette demands that no one start eating until the hostess does. However, if for any reason you are delayed, do invite your guests to start without you: 'I won't be a second, don't let it get cold' will gloss over a potentially awkward moment while you put a finishing touch to the next course in the kitchen.

Awkward food

Try not to serve anything that is going to be problematic to eat. Most people can cope with spaghetti bolognese, and it is likely to be served in a situation where a *little* bit of slurping won't cause offence. If, however, you are serving Chinese food, don't assume that everyone is comfortable using chopsticks: ask if anyone would prefer a fork and ask in such a way that no one is embarrassed to say yes.

> *Try not to serve anything that is going to be problematic to eat.*

Some foods – snails, oysters or globe artichokes, for example – may flummox someone who has never eaten them before. If you choose to serve anything like this, make sure you have mastered the technique so that guests can follow your lead.

A tip for guests in this situation: if in doubt, copy the hostess. If that doesn't help, ask. A self-deprecating question along the lines of 'I'm sorry to be a pleb, but what am I supposed to do here?' will probably have other guests heaving a sigh of relief.

It has been said many times that it is almost impossible to eat corn on the cob elegantly. Some say that it shouldn't be done in public at all. Her Ladyship happens to love corn on the cob and thinks that this is one instance in which elegance may be sacrificed for the sake of enjoyment. She recommends using fingers rather than the little forks designed for the purpose, which are often too flimsy to be useful and generally more trouble than they are worth.

If you are serving anything that must be eaten with the fingers – and even if you can force yourself to scrape the meat off a spare rib with a knife and fork, there is no cutlery that can do justice to a globe artichoke – supply fingerbowls so that guests can rinse their fingers rather than making their napkins too dirty to be usable halfway through the meal. For a formal occasion invest in enough attractive small bowls to supply one for each person; in a less formal setting it is permissible to have two or three larger ones, as long as they are conveniently placed on the table, so that no one has to stretch very far. Fill the bowls no more than half full with warm (not hot) water and add a slice of lemon or a few scented leaves or rose petals to help keep it fresh. Sit the bowls on saucers or small plates to prevent splashes on the table.

Between courses

Aim to have the main course ready to serve almost as soon as the first course is finished. A delay of five minutes while vegetables are steamed or sauce heated is fine; much more is likely to have guests feeling a bit impatient and possibly drinking too much in order to pass the time.

A longer delay between main course and pudding or cheese is not only acceptable, it may be positively welcomed. Those with small appetites can pause for breath while smokers disappear for a few minutes (see box below).

In either case, clear away plates and serving dishes that are finished with as soon as everyone has finished eating. No one likes sitting staring at dirty crockery, and worrying about trailing your sleeve in a gravy-stained plate when you reach for your wine glass can act as a damper to conversation.

A note about smoking

In a non-smoking household, there is no obligation at all to allow anyone to smoke indoors and it would be a very rude guest who 'lit up' without asking permission. However, in the interests of making guests feel comfortable, try to provide a convenient smoking area: outside the back door, on the balcony or wherever it may be. Provide ashtrays to prevent guests having to stub out cigarettes on the lawn or in window boxes. Her Ladyship saves small glass or pottery dishes that once held pâté or chocolate mousse and finds that these work admirably as occasional ashtrays.

Heavy smokers often like to 'pop outside' after the main course: another reason for not serving anything that will be ruined if it is kept waiting for five minutes.

If things go wrong

With sufficient planning and a not overly ambitious menu (see page 92), nothing should go wrong. Even so, timing can sometimes go awry: something that the recipe says should take 20 minutes doesn't look 'done'. If this happens, offer more drinks, replenish nibbles and let whatever it is cook for another few minutes, keeping a very close eye to make sure it doesn't burn or dry out.

If it will boost your confidence, plan (in advance) a fallback position: have a supply of tomatoes, mozzarella and avocados that can be sliced quickly to provide an alternative starter; some frozen vegetables to replace those charred peppers; or enough raspberries to go round if the pudding collapses.

Most importantly of all, do not panic. By all means apologise for a delay – but only once. Your guests are here to enjoy your company, not to see you reduced to a state of abject humiliation through having failed to achieve perfection. In any case, most

By all means apologise for a delay – but only once.

people would rather wait a few minutes longer for good food than eat something underdone but according to schedule.

Far worse than disasters with the food are disasters with the guests. Although, Her Ladyship is glad to say, these are rare occurrences, even the most careful of hostesses may sometimes make an error of judgement and invite people who take a dislike to each other and do not have the manners to conceal it.

If a genuine argument breaks out, intervene as subtly but firmly as possible. You may find it useful to rise to your feet and ask, more loudly than would normally be necessary, whether anyone would like more pudding, coffee or whatever may be appropriate to the stage of the meal. (Offering more wine may add fuel to the already blazing flames and is probably not the best strategy in these circumstances.) If this tactic fails to calm the combatants, a remark addressed specifically to one of them is the next ploy: 'Jeremy, I'm sorry to interrupt, but I've been meaning to talk to you about...' If necessary, ask one of the offending parties to exchange seats with you so that you can sit next to the other and pursue this imaginary line of conversation.

At the end of the meal

Whether you serve coffee at the dining table or move back to the living room is entirely up to you. When making this decision it is worth considering:

• **How comfortable your dining chairs are.** Does it look as if people would rather move to something softer?

• **What sort of state the living room is in.** If it is cluttered with martini glasses and half-eaten bowls of peanuts, you might prefer to stay where you are.

• **How the conversation is going.** Don't disturb people unnecessarily if they are obviously enjoying themselves. On the other hand, with a large group moving may give people the chance to talk to someone who has been sitting at the opposite end of the table.

And, while on the subject of coffee, whatever your own tastes, be aware that many people now prefer to avoid caffeinated drinks in the evening. Offer decaffeinated coffee or tea and perhaps peppermint or camomile tea as well.

Time to go home

Even the most hospitable of hostesses sometimes finds herself longing for her guests to go home. Formal, written invitations indicate the hour at which guests are expected to leave (see page 87), but on less formal occasions a hint can be dropped into the invitation to convey the message. For a midweek supper to which people are coming straight from work, saying, 'I thought it would be better if you came early, since we all have to get up in the morning' has a clear subtext of going home early too.

If guests have not taken that hint, an offer of more coffee when the cups have been sitting empty for a while will often provoke the desired response of 'No, thanks, we ought to be going', and when one person says this others often follow suit. They may have been unwilling to be the first to leave, lest they give the impression of not having enjoyed themselves.

Solicitous questions such as 'What time is the last bus?', 'May I call you a taxi?' or 'Are you happy with your babysitter?' are useful if the time has come to abandon

Only as a last resort should the hostess start yawning and telling people about the early start she has the next day.

subtlety. Only as a last resort should the hostess start yawning and telling people about the early start she has the next day; and only when that has failed should she disappear into her bedroom, return in her dressing gown and bid people a fond good night.

Speaking of taxis, if you don't live in an area where flagging one down in the street is an easy and safe thing to do, make sure you have the telephone number of a reliable firm. If a guest (particularly a lone female one) is happy to go home by public transport or to take a chance on finding a taxi just outside your door, it is polite to escort her to the bus stop and stay until the bus comes, or to wait until an available taxi appears. Remember that, however comfortable your area seems to you, someone who is 'off their normal patch' may feel nervous in the street after dark.

After they've gone

The invention of the dishwasher has made clearing up after guests have gone home much less of a chore than it once was. The most labour-saving approach is to load it as you go along: that is, put the dishes from the starter and main course into the dishwasher when you remove them from the table. Her Ladyship sees no objection to doing this even when guests are eating in the kitchen: she prefers to get mess out of the way than to leave it lying around, however neatly it may be stacked. If guests are in another room and the party is large enough to justify it, it may even be possible to run the dishwasher after the main course, leaving only pudding and cheese dishes, coffee cups and glasses to be dealt with once everyone has left.

However late it is, it is always – always – worth taking the time to clear and if necessary wipe down the table, gather up table cloths and napkins ready for the washing machine, scrape odd bits of cheese or fruit peelings into the bin and load the dishwasher again. Ensure that any leftover food has cooled to room temperature before putting it in the fridge or freezer, but bear in mind that it is unhealthy to leave it out on the worktop overnight. Any washing up that needs to be done by hand should either be done at once or left tidily by the sink. There is nothing worse than walking into the kitchen the following morning and realising that you have left it in a mess – unless it is walking into the living room or dining room and having the same reaction.

Expressions of thanks

The formal thank-you letter is largely a thing of the past, although Her Ladyship is always gratified to receive one. Attitudes to expressions of thanks are largely generational, and here Her Ladyship's advice is for the younger generation to consider the standards and expectations of the older, and the older generation to bear in mind the habits of the younger. Thus a young person who has been to dinner with an aunt or godmother might like to think of writing a card the next day; the lady in question should recognise that this will probably not cross the youngster's mind.

A note to young guests, however: the worst thing that any hostess can receive after extending hospitality is silence. She is likely to worry that her guest was bored rigid, was mugged on the way home, went down with food poisoning in the night, took mortal offence at something the hostess said or any combination of the four. A text indicating that you enjoyed yourself and reached home safely is very much better than nothing.

Hostesses who feel their guests may be lax in this regard could consider sending an email, text or other electronic communication saying, 'Thank you so much for coming and I hope you reached home safely.' This should provoke a response, however brief, and reassure her that not all of the four anxieties mentioned above are justified.

And the next time...

Those who take their entertaining seriously may like to keep records of their dinner parties, both for the fun of it and to avoid repetition. Hostess diaries are sold at exorbitant prices in stationery shops of the better sort, but are an unnecessary extravagance. Any form of notebook will suffice. Things you may like to note for each occasion are:

• **Names of guests** (a useful reminder of who has met whom).

• **Food and wine served** (to avoid repetition when the same people come again).

• **Any likes or dislikes** (there are certain foods, notably beetroot, of which Her Ladyship is very fond but which she would never serve without checking that her guests were of the same mind. A record such as this saves endless re-asking of the same questions).

It is also worth noting a general impression of success or failure: were certain dishes particularly successful? Did the guests like each other? No hostess is likely to need reminding of the sort of guest disaster described on page 109, but the fact that Rachel and Helen got on very well or that the conversation between Mark and Stephen was a bit laboured may not be etched quite so deeply on her memory.

Returning hospitality

…should be done, but need not be done slavishly. Anyone who works or has children or elderly parents or other demands on their time understands that there are occasions when entertaining is simply not an option. Under these circumstances, friends who want to visit should be happy with the simplest of meals or a takeaway – they want to see you, remember? Friends who turn up their noses at such offerings are not real friends and, in Her Ladyship's view, are welcome to stay away.

There are also circumstances in which it is more convenient for one person regularly to host and another regularly to be the guest: when one is older and finds travelling difficult, or has small children and no reliable babysitter; or when one lives centrally and is on the other's route home from work.

The important thing is not to become – or give the appearance of being – a scrounger. If your reason for not entertaining is lack of confidence in your cooking, invite someone to a restaurant as your guest, and make absolutely certain that you pay the bill. This may also be the best approach if the guests are business associates: the conversation need not then be interrupted by your frequent disappearing into the kitchen.

If considerations are financial, consider inviting people for something less lavish (see Chapter 6, *It Doesn't Have to Be Dinner*). If it is a matter of location – you live somewhere difficult to get to – suggest lunch on a Sunday, when guests can be relaxed about the journey home. If none of these is a suitable option, make a point of arriving armed with gifts that are more personal than a bunch of flowers gleaned hastily from the local garage. Your friends and even some of your relatives should be pleased to see you whether or not you bring expensive chocolates, but nobody likes a parasite.

Six

IT DOESN'T HAVE
TO BE DINNER

It was always the same every year; I always came down by the same train, arriving at tea-time, and always found Aunt Sadie and the children round the table... It was always the same table and the same tea-things; the china with large roses on it, the tea-kettle and the silver dish for scones simmering over little flames.

Nancy Mitford, *The Pursuit of Love*, 1945

Although afternoon tea is not the ritual it once was, it remains an excellent way for the non-cook to extend hospitality; the more modern institution of brunch, particularly at weekends, is another. Both offer plenty of scope for the imagination without the pressures of the dinner party described in the previous chapter. A visit to the local delicatessen or bakery, or the relevant counters of the better supermarkets, can supply spring rolls and samosas, bagels, cream cheese and smoked salmon, muffins and beautifully decorated cupcakes. These can be served at the dining table, in the living room with plenty of side tables, in the kitchen or in the garden. If the food is simple enough, people can eat standing up and with their fingers. If budget is not an issue, many supermarkets and specialist outlets offer 'party services' that do the vast majority of the work for you.

When the food is uncomplicated (or prepared by someone else) you may like to devote your energies to choosing particularly pretty plates, cups and napkins, or arranging tables and chairs in the garden, or decorating the table with a vase of fresh or dried flowers. The clashing of scents mentioned on page 102 is less important with cold food.

Informal occasions such as these are the best way to accommodate a number of different generations: children are not obliged to sit politely at the table while the grown-ups linger over wine and conversation, and elderly friends and relatives can be given a comfortable chair away from too much hullabaloo. From quite a young age children (not necessarily your own) can be made to feel involved by being asked to hand round trays of food or make sure that Granny has everything she wants.

Buck's fizz (orange juice with sparkling wine) is the traditional accompaniment to brunch. Kir royale (replacing the orange juice with a blackcurrant liqueur) is a stylish alternative. Don't waste vintage champagne on these concoctions. A cheaper cava or prosecco serves the purpose well and will go some way towards appeasing those who believe that adulterating decent wine with fruit juice is an abomination. On the other hand, it is worth splashing out on really good-quality fresh orange juice, or going to the trouble of squeezing it yourself.

> *Buck's fizz (orange juice with sparkling wine) is the traditional accompaniment to brunch.*

With afternoon tea, there is no need to offer anything other than tea or coffee. However, having a choice of teas – Earl Grey, lapsang souchong and/or a herbal variety as well as the more everyday kind – will show your guests that you have made an effort.

A note here for imaginative hostesses: remember that not everybody likes the more scented teas. Remember also that the essence of hospitality is to make your guests feel comfortable, so try not to be disappointed if you are asked for 'ordinary tea' when you have gone to the trouble of procuring several more exotic kinds. The same applies to cocktail parties (see page 123) – some people would genuinely prefer a 'straight' glass of wine to any gorgeous concoction you may have on offer.

Barbecues

...always seem like a good idea on a sunny summer's day, but are fraught with difficulty for the novice. First, the charcoal takes an age to heat up, meaning that you can't begin cooking until an hour later than you anticipated. Second, if the heat is not exactly right, food such as chicken and sausages that needs to be cooked through will be charred on the outside while still unhealthily pink within. Third, in Britain at least, there is no guarantee that what started out as the brightest of mornings may not be grey, windy and miserable by early afternoon. Or occasionally it may turn uncomfortably hot.

Her Ladyship therefore offers the following tips:

• **Most importantly,** *just don't do it* **if you are not competent.** Practise on family or small numbers of close friends first. Rather than put guests through the agony of watching you get it wrong, offer a buffet meal prepared in the kitchen and laid out on an indoor table. Guests can help themselves and sit outside if the weather permits.

• **If only a barbecue will do,** check the day before that the equipment is clean and that all the necessary tools are to hand. Start heating before the guests arrive. Some modern barbecues go from ambient temperature to ready-to-grill in ten minutes; many others do not and it is misjudging this stage of the proceedings that causes the most vexation.

• **Marinate meat such as spare ribs the evening before** and leave it overnight in the fridge. If the very thought of this causes you to panic, you will almost certainly find a section in a good supermarket where this part of the work has been done for you.

• **Prepare a variety of salads in advance.** Mrs Beeton's advice on this subject holds good to this day: 'Salads afford considerable scope for the exercise of individual taste and inventive faculty, and whatever their composition, they should always look cool, inviting, and dainty.' The best salads of Her Ladyship's experience are made by a friend who dislikes both tomatoes and cucumbers and has to use her imagination rather than falling back on these staples. Colour may be introduced by red peppers, sweetcorn or the odd leaf of radicchio; interest added (probably not all at once) by avocado, asparagus, green beans, walnuts, cubes of cheese, prawns or hard-boiled egg; and the whole topped with leaves of fresh basil or mint.

• **Strawberries or other seasonal fruits make an ample dessert.**
If you want to offer something more substantial, consider something like a supermarket *tarte au citron*. Avoid creamy or chocolaty puddings, which tend to slump into an unattractive goo when the weather is hot.

• **Fill a coolbox or large plastic container with ice**, beer and other drinks to be served chilled. Keep it outside in a shady place so that guests requiring replenishment don't have far to go.

• **Particularly on a hot day, make sure you can offer plenty of water or soft drinks.**

• **Make provision for people who prefer to sit in the shade.** Erect sun umbrellas, put cushions under trees or simply make sure there is somewhere for them to sit indoors without missing out on the entire party.

• **Be considerate of the neighbours.** Try to avoid filling their gardens with smoke and bear in mind that what to the participants is the happy sound of good friends having a convivial time may be an intolerable intrusion to someone wanting a quiet afternoon with the Sunday papers. Warn them a few days in advance that you are contemplating an outdoor party and express the polite hope that it won't disturb them too much. If it is a special occasion such as a birthday or anniversary, tell them so: they are more likely to be tolerant if you have assured them (truthfully) that this doesn't happen often. You could even minimise the risk of complaints by inviting them.

Drinks parties

… sound straightforward but can be difficult to make a success of: the balance of food and drink is a delicate one to maintain. Particularly with an early evening party, when people have had nothing to eat since lunchtime, you need to supply enough food to absorb the alcohol that your guests are bound to consume. Caterers recommend anything from ten to fifteen small canapés per person for a party lasting two hours, depending on whether you think of them as appetisers or as adding together to form a light meal.

If you don't feel up to making your own, good supermarkets do an excellent range of 'party food' from all over the world. For special occasions, this is the one time when Her Ladyship would consider splashing out on a caterer. It is a rare hostess who can prepare bite-sized Yorkshire puddings with a sliver of beef and horseradish the way the professionals do.

The amount of drink needed depends on how much you expect people to consume and how many of them are driving. In cities where public transport or taxis are abundant, Her Ladyship recommends as much as a bottle of wine per head. In rural areas, half this amount would probably be sufficient, though it is always better to over- than to under-cater. Most wine merchants will offer sale-or-return facilities. They will also lend or hire glasses and sell ice. Whether in addition to wine you offer beer and/or spirits is up to you, your budget and your knowledge of your guests' tastes. However, you should always have a plentiful supply of soft drinks – mineral water, orange juice and perhaps something more interesting such as elderflower cordial or a non-alcoholic punch.

If you enjoy mixing cocktails and think your friends will appreciate them, you could offer bellinis (sparkling wine with peach juice), margaritas (usually tequila, cointreau and lime, though Her Ladyship once drank a delicious strawberry version in a West Indian restaurant in New York), mojitos (rum, sugar, lime and mint) or anything else that takes your fancy. An inventive friend of Her Ladyship's once gave a party in which guests mixed their own throughout the evening: she provided the ingredients and recipes for six cocktails, plus glasses, bendy straws, umbrellas and plenty of fruit for decoration. It was Christmas and guests were in a festive spirit. They happily experimented, relieving the hostess of the need to ensure that everyone's drink was kept topped up.

Be warned, though: cocktails (particularly those with innuendo-laden names) can be very alcoholic and are all too easy to drink. Those used to calculating that a small glass of wine contains one or two units of alcohol can find they have sloshed down six or more units in an alarmingly short space of time. The caring hostess will provide plenty of suitable food (much of it bread-based) to counterbalance this.

The other disadvantage of cocktail parties is that you find yourself left with half a bottle of tequila and a third of rum which you would never drink under any other circumstances. These either clutter up the drinks cupboard for years to come or provide an excellent excuse for another party.

Dealing with mess

At drinks parties this is another potential worry. Most of Her
Ladyship's friends, seated at a dinner table and provided with a
knife and fork, can be relied upon to spill nothing more serious
than breadcrumbs on the floor. The same cannot be said when
they are standing up, clutching a glass of wine and a napkin in one
hand and trying to dip a cocktail sausage in barbecue sauce with
the other. If your carpet is precious and/or likely to show stains, it
is well worth investing in some cheaper and darker covering for
the occasion. This is also sound practice if you have a hardwood
floor, which may be damaged by stiletto heels. If you feel strongly
about it, check the proposed menu and dispense with anything
greasy. One particularly house-proud friend of Her Ladyship's
goes so far as to refuse to serve red wine at her drinks parties, but
most people would think this was carrying precautionary measures
too far. In olden times, carpets – which were not fitted as they are
now, but were effectively room-sized rugs – were rolled out of the
way to produce dance floors for parties, but this is a task that
requires an army of footmen or willing volunteers, not to mention
somewhere to put the carpet during the festivities, and will not be
practicable for many hostesses.

Whatever your attitude to your carpet and to the footwear
of family members or weekend guests, do not on any account ask
guests to remove their shoes. It is only courteous to assume that
they left home with clean shoes; in addition, the effect of many
outfits will be ruined if they are not accompanied by high heels.
If the weather is bad and/or you live at the end of a muddy
country lane, you can expect people to arrive in 'outdoor' shoes
and to change them as soon as they arrive. In these circumstances,
provide somewhere for them to leave shoes just as you do for coats
and umbrellas.

A cautionary tale about carpets

In a fit of youthful enthusiasm when buying her first home, Her Ladyship chose for the living room a completely impractical pale blue 'velvet' carpet. Even the shop from which she bought it advised against it and a wise friend warned, 'When you buy a carpet, you have to imagine what it's going to look like when someone's just spilt a cup of coffee on it.' As it happens, the first thing to be spilt was a glass of port, though this says more about Her Ladyship's friends than it does about the carpet. That stain never came out and the carpet, not designed to withstand normal levels of living-room wear and tear, looked shabby from a very early stage.

Her Ladyship knows better now – and has given many more parties since. She tells this anecdote as a warning that you are going to cause yourself unnecessary grief if you invest in impractical things and don't acknowledge the fact that they are impractical.

Seven

WEEKEND VISITORS
AND THE WEEKEND HOME

Don't presume on [your host's] kindness by attempting to stay beyond what he presses you to do, for two short visits tell better than one long one, looking as though you have been approved of. You can easily find out from the butler or the groom of the chambers, or some of the upper servants, how long you are expected to stay.

R S Surtees, *Ask Mamma*, 1858

As with inviting people to dinner, having people to stay should be a pleasure. You should exert yourself to make sure guests are comfortable and feel at home – but not so much that the operation becomes a source of resentment.

Again as with inviting people to dinner, a crucial first step is to make clear what is included in an invitation. No one relishes coming home at the end of a busy week to **A crucial first step** find guests already camped out on the **is to make clear** doorstep. Her Ladyship remembers with **what is included** gratitude an occasion when a friend, **in an invitation.** arriving early and finding no one in, sat in her car across the street, watched Her Ladyship come home, waited and rang the doorbell a full half-hour later. By then Her Ladyship – unaware and therefore unhassled – had had time to unpack the shopping, wash, change her clothes, check that there were clean towels on the spare bed and perform myriad other small tasks that would have been more awkward once a guest had arrived. Such courtesy is distressingly rare and should be much encouraged. The advent of mobile phones has, of course, made it easier to inform a host or a guest that one is running early or late, but given the choice between the two one should always arrive (slightly) after the appointed time.

These considerations are doubled and redoubled if you are inviting friends to your weekend home (see page 138). If you tend to arrive there frazzled and fractious at nine o'clock on Friday night, it might be prudent to suggest guests arrive in time for Saturday lunch.

To return to the subject of invitations, these are normally informal, issued verbally or by email, making it appropriate to say something like 'I normally get home about seven, so give me half an hour.' (This should, of course, be used only if you normally get home about half-past six.) As to the vexed question of when guests are to leave, 'We'll do brunch on Sunday, so you can drift off whenever you're ready' tells a weekend guest that the hostess would like Sunday afternoon to herself, and is likely to be welcome news to anyone who has to work on Monday. Alternatively, 'Stay for lunch on Sunday' allows the guest to linger a bit into the afternoon but makes it clear that they should not expect to stay for supper.

The guest bedroom

It is a mistake, unless your guests are of the age and disposition to sleep on the floor, to invite more people than can comfortably be accommodated in bedrooms. You can make an exception to this rule if you have a large garden with a comfortable summer house, or perhaps a caravan parked somewhere on the property, but even then serious consideration must be given to temperature and to bathroom facilities. Many spare bedrooms double as home offices, so it may not cause disruption to have someone sleeping there on Friday and Saturday, but becomes inconvenient if they are staying until Monday. Teenage children may be evicted from their bedrooms in order to accommodate weekend guests but, given that they are likely to sleep until lunch time, they should not be allocated the living-room floor or sofa unless the adults of the party are intending to go out for the day or you have a choice of living-rooms in which to entertain them.

If, as hostess, you are in any doubt as to whether or not your guests wish to share a room, you *must* find a tactful way to ask before they arrive unless you have so many spare bedrooms that you can segregate them at short notice. If someone you know well is bringing a new 'friend' for the first time, it is potentially embarrassing for all concerned – and therefore the worst of ill manners – to assume that they are on intimate terms. If the house is crowded, single people of the same sex and roughly the same age can be asked to share a twin room, but should not be expected to share a bed. However, most people of forty-plus would be uncomfortable being asked to share with someone in their twenties whom they didn't know well, and vice versa.

It should go without saying that guest bedrooms should be freshly dusted and vacuumed, and that bed linen should be clean. Particularly in winter, make sure that there is plenty of bedding. If in doubt, leave an extra blanket or bedspread on a chair or in the wardrobe so that guests can put it on the bed if they feel cold – and point it out to them when they arrive. As an 1890s edition of *Good Housekeeping* wisely pointed out, 'Nothing is so vexatious as for a guest to find, on preparing to retire, that the bed is lightly clothed... Most guests are reluctant to ask for more bedding, especially when left alone, with the probability that all others in the house may have gone to bed; so they either lie and shiver through a considerable portion of the night, or are driven to other expedients for obtaining the essential degree of warmth.' Her

Ladyship glosses lightly over the question of what those 'other expedients' might be, but feels that the point is nonetheless an important one.

Clean towels should await the guests, either on the bed or on the towel rail in their bathroom (see below). A small basket of toiletries, a few flowers in a pretty vase, a flask of fresh water and a glass by the bed are considerate touches. There should be a small table with a lamp beside the bed (on both sides if it is a double bed for double occupancy) – the guest who likes to read in bed should not have to get up in order to put out the light. If you choose to leave a few books or magazines on the bedside table – another welcoming gesture – bear in mind that a guest who casually picks up a book on Friday night may be engrossed in it by Sunday morning: never leave out anything that you are not prepared to lend for a while.

> *Clean towels should await the guests, either on the bed or on the towel rail in their bathroom.*

The wardrobe should have enough space and spare hangers for guests to hang three or four items each. In the absence of a wardrobe, make sure that there are hangers on a hook on the back of the door or invest in a 'clothes valet', a stand with rails at various heights on which garments may be hung. These stands need not be expensive and there are collapsible varieties that can be stored away between guests.

If the guest bedroom can accommodate it, provide tea- and coffee-making facilities and offer a jug of milk immediately before your guests retire. This prevents early risers having to fumble round in an unfamiliar kitchen and disturbing those of less matutinal habits.

If at all possible, guests should have a bathroom to themselves. If not, they should be given an indication of the household's morning routine. Telling a visitor, 'We normally get up about nine' enables the host and hostess to rise at half-past eight and use the bathroom before the guests are likely to want it. Guests should, of course, never take possession of a shared bathroom for more than a very few minutes without checking that it is convenient to everyone else.

Always prepare guest bedrooms and bathrooms in advance, so that when your visitors arrive you can show them to their rooms and invite them to make themselves comfortable. Show them where things are kept and point out any oddities such as low ceilings, unexpected steps and the fact that the shower has to be switched on outside the bathroom. Then, having made sure that they know their way around and promised them appropriate refreshment as soon as they are ready to join you, leave them to wash, unpack and relax at their leisure.

The weekend routine

Her Ladyship does not advise making any formal or inflexible plans for Friday evening if guests are coming for the weekend. They may arrive late, exhausted after a hard week and distressed by traffic; it is both courteous and practical to have a relaxed attitude to the evening meal. Something like lasagne or chilli can be prepared in advance and reheated when the guests arrive with no suggestion that it will spoil if they are late. Sophisticated culinary efforts can and should wait until Saturday.

It is worth owning a supply of distinctive napkin rings so that, after Friday supper, everyone can roll up their own and use it again at breakfast. If Saturday dinner or Sunday lunch is to be more formal, provide clean napkins, but there is no need for this the rest of the time.

If plans for Saturday require rising, and possibly departing the house, at a certain time, make this clear on Friday night. If, for example, you are planning a visit to the races, say something like

'We want to be there at eleven, so we should leave here at ten. Breakfast about half-past eight, then?' If there is a good reason for wanting to be there at eleven – perhaps because it will be impossible to park if you are late or because you have a horse running in the first race – make this clear. Polite guests will fall in with this arrangement. If, on the other hand, the schedule is not really important (parking isn't a problem and your horse isn't running until the fourth race) and you can tell by their look of poorly suppressed dismay that half-past eight is very early for Saturday breakfast, be accommodating. No host/ess should cram the weekend so full of engagements that guests have no time to rest; nor should they plan to go to the races or anywhere else without first checking that this is something the guests would enjoy.

After a day out, there should be a lull of an hour or so before the evening's entertainment. During this time host and guests alike may choose to retire to their rooms to rest, or to relax on the sofa with the newspaper and a cup of tea. As host/ess you are under no obligation to be at your sparkling best every minute of the day – indeed, by this stage your guests will almost certainly appreciate being given some time out.

This is particularly likely to be the case if you invite a single person into a busy family household, or older people into a house full of children and pets. Be sensitive to the fact that, however charming guests may find the difference between their lifestyle and yours, they may also find it exhausting after a while.

The weekend wardrobe

It is a courtesy to guests to tell them of any plans for which they should come prepared. Some city dwellers, for example, assume that no one who lives in the country wears anything other than sweaters and jeans, and may be embarrassed to find they have been invited to a dinner party. Conversely, other city dwellers have no concept of mud or livestock, and may need to be reminded to bring suitable footwear for a country walk. If you happen to own a swimming pool or a tennis court, again, suggest to guests that they bring suitable clothing.

Children and dogs

In households where there are children in residence, it is normally no problem for guests to bring their own. Indeed, it is unrealistic to expect them not to. Even child-free homes should expect to include children in invitations for the weekend. Those who for whatever reason (whether lack of space or unconquerable allergy to children) feel they cannot accommodate their friends' offspring but do not want to offend the parents can say something along the lines of 'I'd love to invite you for the weekend but we just don't have the room for you all'. Parents who are eager to accept the invitation will read between the lines: they can then offer to stay in a nearby bed and breakfast or suggest a date when the children have other plans. (Anyone with small children will be aware that the average five-year-old has a much more active social life than its parents do.) However, it is an unbreachable point of etiquette that it is up to the parents to suggest they leave the children in the care of a grandparent or friend rather than for the hostess to hint that the younger generation would not be welcome.

Note that this does not apply to wedding invitations. A bride and groom are perfectly within their rights to opt for an 'adults only' occasion.

Small children are an exception to the 'don't invite them if you don't have the space' rule. They can share beds with the resident children, or sleep on the floor of the children's room. It doesn't matter if they talk and giggle half the night unless, perhaps, they are performing in a concert the next day. If you live next door to the Royal Albert Hall and the prodigies' parents have begged you to provide emergency accommodation, this may be cause for concern; otherwise, you are safe to relax and let the little ones enjoy themselves.

Dogs are a separate issue. Dogs are welcome only if your home is able and you are willing to accommodate them and the dog owner takes full responsibility for all their needs. A friend of Her Ladyship's reports inviting friends plus dog to stay in her second-floor flat, an experience that could have been traumatic. In fact, after a brief sniff around the dog ate his dinner (brought, along with his dish and water bowl, by his owners), settled down peacefully and slept all evening. His owners took him out last thing at night and unobtrusively rose early the next morning to do the same. They even asked for a broom to sweep the kitchen floor before breakfast, lest the dog's hair cause annoyance. All the hostess had to do, apart from providing the broom, was to supply a spare key so that dog and owners could come and go from the flat as they pleased.

These are well-trained dog-owners and a well-trained dog. It also happens that Her Ladyship's friend likes dogs. This combination of circumstances may not apply to you or to your friends' dogs. The non-dog-lover is under no obligation to include a dog in her invitation. 'I'm sorry, I can't let you bring Ben, my cleaner is allergic to dogs and I can't afford to upset her' is an unanswerable explanation.

CHILD PROOF AND DOG PROOF

If you aren't used to children and dogs, it can be difficult to predict what might prove a hazard to them. Her Ladyship, warned that a visiting toddler was at the stage of being intrigued by the television's remote control, put it on top of the piano out of the way. Or so she thought. The enterprising youngster spotted it and climbed on to the piano stool to reach it, putting himself in much more danger than if the device had been left in its usual place on the coffee table.

The best advice here is to put away anything that you would not want a dog to chew or a child to spill orange squash on – velvet cushions and hardback books are obvious examples. In other words, protect your own possessions, then rely on the owners/parents to make sure that their dogs and offspring do not come to harm.

Children's behaviour

Her Ladyship is constantly amazed by the number of parents who allow their children to run riot in other people's homes or in restaurants, museums or other public places where such behaviour is inappropriate. She does not mean that children should sit quietly with the adults at all times, but that they should not run screaming up and down corridors (that is why gardens were invented), jump on furniture, interrupt conversations without apology, help themselves to food without asking or otherwise behave like guttersnipes. While most parents will, in fact, endeavour to exercise a modicum of control when taking their children to someone else's home, it may sometimes become necessary for you to intervene in order to protect your possessions or preserve your sanity.

The best approach is simply to ask a child not to do that – whatever 'that' may be. This does not mean imitating Joyce Grenfell's ineffectual 'George, don't do that'. Any of the various television incarnations of Miss Marple, quietly determined to have their own way, would be a better role model. A firm 'We don't do that in *my* house' is an unanswerable reply to 'I'm allowed to do it at home.'

Problems of etiquette

Most weekend visitors are likely to be friends. Why else would you invite them? However, even one's closest friends occasionally have partners you would cross the street to avoid, and spending 48 hours with someone you have only ever spent an evening with before can give rise to unexpected problems. What *do* you do if you find you have invited for the weekend someone whose table manners, personal habits or political views disgust you?

Her Ladyship's view is, 'Grit your teeth and take comfort from the thought that you will never, ever, in any circumstances, ask them again.' This does not, of course, work with in-laws or even one's own relatives, who have an alarming tendency to invite themselves.

However, rather than face a weekend of teeth-gritting (or grinding), Her Ladyship advises evasive action. Somehow, you must keep these people entertained and, with luck, force others to do the lion's share of the entertaining for you. If you have a local pub where you are likely to meet a number of familiar faces, take your guests along and introduce them to everyone you know. Take them to an art exhibition or for a long walk in the park, where conversation can be limited to admiring or criticising the pictures or the scenery.

If you have left it too late to fill every minute with distractions (which under normal circumstances would be undesirable; see page 133) and the weather is keeping everyone indoors in all-too-close proximity, inventing chores or commitments to occupy yourself in another part of the house may be the only answer. 'Would you forgive me if I left you for an hour or so? I must write some letters/finish this report/water the plants in the greenhouse?' should buy you some necessary breathing space. Be sure you have an ally, if only at the end of the phone: telling a friend on Monday 'I got through the weekend without biting that dreadful man's head off' will earn you sympathetic praise and give you a sense of virtuous achievement.

A weekend home

Anyone who is fortunate enough to own a second home knows that it is a responsibility as well as a pleasure. Even if you go there faithfully every weekend, it is as well to have someone to 'keep an eye' in your absence. A benevolent neighbour may be happy to check for frozen pipes in cold weather and to ensure that there is no mail protruding from the letter box to tell passing burglars that the place is empty. If, however, your visits are sporadic or you require more of a commitment than that, it may be worth employing an agent to do routine maintenance such as mowing the lawn. That way, you are able to relax and enjoy when you do visit, rather than spend precious time doing chores.

Anyone who is fortunate enough to own a second home knows that it is a responsibility as well as a pleasure.

There are strong arguments for hiring a professional to do this work. Asking a neighbour to do a favour every now and again is all very well, but you should consider what would happen if something went wrong. Far better to fall out with a stranger (whom you can, if necessary, sue without causing ill feeling in the village) than to become estranged from a neighbour and force others to take sides.

How fully equipped a second home needs to be depends on how often you are going to be there, how comfortable you want to be, how much you are going to entertain and whether you travel to it by car or public transport.

In an ideal world, the second home – and particularly the kitchen and bathroom – should be as fully equipped as your main residence. It is, after all, a home: you should not feel that you are camping there. Nor should you feel obliged to carry towels and oven gloves every time you go away for the weekend, or be restricted as to what you can cook for dinner because of the absence of a cheese grater or asparagus steamer. Specifically, Her Ladyship suggests:

• **Keeping a full set of cosmetics** and toiletries and duplicating any necessary medicines.

• **Making friends with the local farm shop** and arranging to have a vegetable box delivered on a Friday afternoon.

• **Keeping at least the sort of wardrobe** you might take on a two-week holiday, allowing for changes of weather, impromptu invitations and the spilling of red wine.

In all these instances, the mantra is 'What would it be really irritating to find myself without?' If you enjoy baking and the weekend in the country is the only time that you can indulge this pleasure, a ready supply of icing sugar and vanilla extract may assume a great deal more importance than you would ever have thought possible.

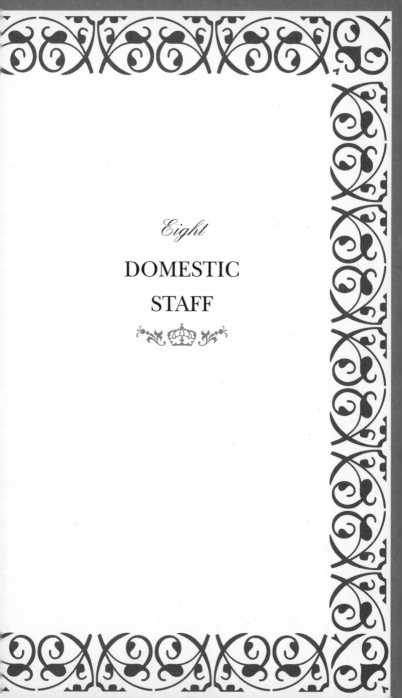

Eight

DOMESTIC
STAFF

It had undoubtedly helped a man in his dealings with the domestic staff to have…the rights of the high, the middle and the low justice – which meant, broadly, that if you got annoyed with your head-gardener you could immediately divide him into four head-gardeners with a battle-axe and no questions asked.

P G Wodehouse, *Blandings Castle and Elsewhere,* 1935

Before embarking on advice on dealing with staff, Her Ladyship would like to offer some reassurance to the twenty-first-century homemaker. While women of an earlier generation were daunted by the prospect of dealing with all their housework without domestic help, those brought up in the era of superwomen and hyper-achievers may feel a sense of failure if they *don't* cope with everything themselves. Her Ladyship firmly believes that, for the modern working woman, this is nonsense. There is no shame attached to paying someone to do a job you don't have the time, inclination or expertise to do yourself. A busy person who hires someone else to walk the dog or do the gardening and spends that time earning the money to pay for this perceived luxury will be less stressed, more fulfilled and probably financially better off than if she grudgingly shoe-horns these tasks into an already overstuffed schedule. She will also have a healthier dog and a tidier garden.

Reverting to P G Wodehouse's lament, however, it is Her Ladyship's view that getting annoyed with your head gardener, or anyone else who works for you – certainly to the point of setting about them with a battle-axe – is a luxury few modern-day employers can afford. Mrs Beeton's advice on the subject is rather more practical:

> *Good temper should be cultivated by every mistress, as upon it the welfare of the household may be said to turn; indeed, its influence can hardly be over-estimated, as it has the effect of moulding the characters of those around her, and of acting most beneficially on the happiness of the domestic circle.*

By mistress, of course, she means 'housewife and employer of servants' rather than any more modern sense of the word, although the advice may be sound in that context too.

Good help is like gold dust and many women would no more willingly share their cleaner with a friend than they would their hairdresser. That said, if you *can* worm a recommendation out of your friends or neighbours, it is the best way to find reliable cleaners, gardeners, window cleaners, chimney sweeps and myriad others. As a second choice, those living in cities are constantly bombarded by business cards through the letter box offering cleaning, decorating and other domestic services. Many diligent and reliable people can be discovered by following these up.

Mrs Beeton, advising her readers on the taking up of references, recommends a face-to-face conversation with the former employer, on the basis that if she is not smart and clean, her servant may have picked up bad habits. Her Ladyship would agree that this is the ideal approach, but recognises that in today's world it is not always practical. The telephone is the next best thing: email offers no opportunity to gauge the referee's standards and general attitudes.

However, not every would-be domestic can offer references. Some are recently arrived in the country; others may have embarked only lately on this line of work. In such cases, Her Ladyship recommends a morning's or a day's 'trial' without commitment on either side. At the end of this period you will be able to judge if the work has been done well and have a feeling for whether or not you like and trust the person concerned. The latter is crucial, of course, because you are likely to give a cleaner the keys to your home so that she can come and go while you are at work. Imagine trying to explain to your insurance company that you gave your keys to a complete stranger, went out with a promise not to return for eight hours and came back to find your silver and jewellery missing.

In the interests of presenting a balanced view, however, it should be pointed out that a trial period also gives the potential employee time to draw her own conclusions about what sort of taskmistress you are likely to be.

The next stage...

... is explaining what you want someone to do. Mrs Beeton offers this sound advice:

> We would here point out an error – and a grave one it is – into which some mistresses fall. They do not, when engaging a servant, expressly tell her all the duties which she will be expected to perform. This is an act of omission severely to be reprehended. Every portion of work which the maid will have to do, should be plainly stated by the mistress, and understood by the servant. If this plan is not carefully adhered to, domestic contention is almost certain to ensue.

An experienced cleaner will need to be told little more than 'Please clean this, please polish that every time' and shown where cleaning materials are kept. Bear in mind, however, that many people clean not because they are good or experienced at it but because it is the only work available to them. They may need guidance on which products to use for which areas and, in the early stages, supervision to make sure the job is being done to your satisfaction. Whether the cleaner is experienced or not, you need to be clear about any personal quirks or anything you think is particularly important: if you suffer from asthma, for example, you probably like the mattress to be vacuumed or brushed more often than others would think necessary.

Equally important is instructing a cleaner what *not* to do. The tedium of cleaning your collection of Meissen shepherdesses yourself more than makes up for the anguish and ill-feeling that arises if one of them is broken.

All the above applies not just to cleaners. One friend of Her Ladyship's, a keen gardener but a busy person, once hired someone to help with the routine maintenance of her garden. She was distraught to come home after a hard day's work to find that her carefully chosen wildflowers had been ruthlessly uprooted by a well-meaning novice who thought they were weeds.

Time and motion

Mrs Beeton was for the most part dealing with live-in, full-time servants. Today you are more likely to be asking someone to work a few hours a week. Even so, the work to be done and the time it is likely to take should be mutually agreed beforehand. If the agreement on a first occasion is that a cleaner works for three hours but she does the work in two and a half because she is quick and efficient, she should be paid for the full three hours. The next time, you might like to have an additional task in readiness to occupy her for the balance of the time if need be.

If, on the other hand, the work takes three and a half hours, you are in a more awkward position. Has the cleaner been absolutely meticulous? Has she taken longer because she is unfamiliar with the house? Or is she just slow? If it is the last of these, think carefully before taking her on: the irritation of thinking 'I could do it myself in half the time' detracts hugely from the relief of having someone else do the work.

If the problem is meticulousness, you are faced with a dilemma. It is very difficult to make a meticulous person be less meticulous, so if she does not speed up on subsequent visits the only solutions may be to have her omit one of the allotted tasks altogether, or to resign yourself to paying her for the extra time. If she is that good, she is probably worth it.

To avoid misunderstandings, the initial briefing *must* be done face to face, as must any follow-up. A friend of Her Ladyship's tells a salutary story of having explained what needed to be done to a new cleaner in person, but then gone out to work. She came home to an immaculately clean house and emailed to ask if the cleaner was happy with the arrangement. What she thought she was asking was, 'Is the three hours we agreed on enough? Did you feel under pressure?' and 'Is three hours too much? Did you get everything done more quickly than that?' Somehow, the cleaner read this as a criticism of her work, took umbrage and never returned.

As a rule of thumb, however, you should employ a cleaner (or a gardener, or anyone else who is paid by the hour) for slightly longer than the time taken to carry out routine work. This means that 'every now and then' tasks such as polishing the silver or clearing out a kitchen cupboard can be fitted in without sacrificing the cleanliness of the bathroom.

Financial arrangements

It is vital that these are mutually agreed before a duster is lifted or rubber glove donned. If necessary, ask around friends and neighbours to find out what the 'going rate' is.

It is a matter of basic courtesy to have any employee's money to hand when the job is done (in cash unless you have specifically arranged otherwise). Very few people clean other people's houses or mow other people's lawns for fun. If you are in a position to employ someone to do your housework or garden for you, you almost certainly have more money than they do. Not being able to pay straight away because you have 'not had time to go to the bank' is evidence of the most overwhelming arrogance on your part.

Friendly terms

In Her Ladyship's view, the temptation to gossip with staff should be resisted. This is particularly important if a cleaner or other help has been recommended by a friend. A cleaner who gossips to you about your friend on Tuesday is unlikely to be discreet when she visits that friend on Thursday.

Of course it goes without saying that you should treat anyone you employ with courtesy. But your relationship is still one of employer/employee. As an experienced

It is wise to be friendly without being friends. friend of Her Ladyship's puts it, it is wise to be friendly without being friends. This may mean listening to the employee's troubles without sharing your own. It may mean

giving help and advice to someone who is less well equipped than you are (because of a language barrier, perhaps) to deal with 'the system'. It may mean allowing a cleaner to bring a child with her during the holidays if her normal child-care arrangements have let her down; it does not mean feeling obliged to spend three hours entertaining the child. And while a small present for birthdays and at Christmas is a friendly gesture, an employee might prefer to see the evidence of your generosity in the form of a cash bonus.

LANGUAGE DIFFICULTIES

… with those who do not have English as their mother tongue can usually be overcome by a combination of common sense, mutual goodwill and pointing or demonstrating. This should, however, stop short of actual acrobatics. A friend of Her Ladyship's was once trying to explain to a new cleaner with limited English that her daughter's dancing kit needed to be dried in a hurry. Her Ladyship cannot help feeling that her friend's energetic mime of the workings of a tumble dryer must only have added to the poor woman's bemusement.

Living in

Ground rules and basic courtesy are even more important when a nanny or au pair lives in. *Au pair*, after all, means 'on a par, equal', not 'general skivvy or factotum'. In Her Ladyship's experience the worst problems in these circumstances arise through a clash of expectations. At one extreme, a host family hopes to employ a maid of all work for minimal payment, while the au pair wants to live somewhere more glamorous than her home town, to go clubbing with others in a similar position and to do as little work as possible. At the other, ideal-world end of the spectrum, a young adult has the opportunity to immerse herself in a different culture, improve her language skills and enjoy herself in a new environment while still making herself useful. Her hosts welcome a new person into their family, give their own children the chance to experience another culture and at the same time have someone on hand to relieve them of some of their domestic burdens. It is not unusual for successful au pair/host relationships to evolve into lifelong friendships. Between these two extremes are probably the majority of perfectly satisfactory but not life-changing experiences.

In the absence of word-of-mouth recommendation, Her Ladyship would always recommend finding an au pair, nanny or mother's help through a reputable agency. Both family and applicant submit a 'personal statement' of requirements and expectations and the agency puts together suitable pairings. Finding the right match can take

In the absence of word-of-mouth recommendation, Her Ladyship would always recommend finding an au pair, nanny or mother's help through a reputable agency.

time, so consider making the initial application three to four months before you want the employment to start.

However carefully the screening and matching process has been done, there are always going to be oddities of culture – little things that nobody thought to mention but that either host family or au pair may find unusual in the other's habits. British homes can seem uncomfortably cold to Scandinavians – one family was amazed to find that their au pair expected to wear only a T-shirt indoors in winter and did not take kindly to their suggestion that she put on a jumper. Wearing shoes indoors, having fitted carpets and eating later in the evening than she was used to are all things that au pairs of Her Ladyship's acquaintance have found strange on their first visit to England.

Flexibility is the watchword for all concerned here: part of the reason for entering into this relationship is to learn about another culture. Although it is reasonable to expect an au pair to be adaptable, you should also be aware that she may be away from home for the first time and try to make her feel as comfortable as possible. Her Ladyship is not, she hastens to add, advocating that her readers go so far as to remove fitted carpets, but feels sure that they grasp the gist of what she is trying to say.

The roles, hours of work and remuneration of au pairs, nannies and mother's helps are defined by guidelines established by the trade association to which reputable agencies belong. Au pairs are expected to do some housework; nannies should clean up after themselves and the children but not after the adult members of the household. Anyone living in should have their own room – comfortably furnished, including a television – and preferably their own bathroom. They take their meals either with the whole family or with the children if these are young enough to eat separately, but should sometimes be invited to join 'grown-up' occasions or outings. When they are off duty their privacy should be respected – that is, they should be left in peace.

Any additional expenses, duties and privileges should be clearly agreed. Although au pairs are expected to do some babysitting, most of them also attend English classes, which are likely to be in the evening: try to arrange your babysitting needs so that they don't clash with her studies. In these days of ubiquitous mobile phones the annoyance of a homesick au pair using your phone to run up huge bills is largely a thing of the past, but you might consider contributing to the cost of her phone. If she is to have the use of a car, make it clear when and under what circumstances; if not, buy her a travel pass or give her a regular sum to cover fares. Remember that au pairs are generally given bed and board and paid 'pocket money' rather than a living wage, so if they are to benefit fully from the experience you will have to contribute to their reasonable expenses.

Having an au pair in your home is in some ways like acquiring a teenage daughter (she may be as young as seventeen), so the sort of ground rules mentioned on page 46–47 need to be established. Of course you must allow her to entertain her friends, but you may not be

Having an au pair in your home is in some ways like acquiring a teenage daughter.

happy about her inviting them to stay the night, or about her staying out all night herself on a night off. Again, this sort of thing needs to be established at an early stage, to avoid misunderstandings and ill feeling.

Mother's helps and nannies tend to be older than au pairs and many come from the UK or from English-speaking Commonwealth countries. The linguistic and cultural differences are therefore reduced, as is the risk that homesickness will make the whole experience an unhappy one. But everything else that Her Ladyship has said about welcoming someone into your home and treating them with respect applies.

CONCLUSION

To sum up, Her Ladyship would like to offer the following golden rules for running a harmonious home within the confines of twenty-first-century reality. If you take nothing else away from this book, please remember these:

• **Don't turn the house into the enemy**. Work out a system that suits your schedule and stick to it as far as is convenient. Yes, it's wonderful to have a clean home, but no one in their right mind turns down an attractive invitation because they are planning to wash the Venetian blinds.

• **Clear up spillages** as soon as they happen. Like cleaning the oven, this is a task that becomes more traumatic if you put it off. Although a number of tried and tested maxims may be applied to housework, 'Ignore it and it'll go away' is not one of them.

• **When it comes to spring-cleaning**, remember that less is less. To paraphrase William Morris (rather loosely, perhaps), if you don't use it or love it, throw it out.

• **With laundry**, follow the instructions on care labels; don't wash yellow dusters or deep-dye towels with white blouses; and remember that delicates are called delicates for a reason. The annoyance you feel when you damage your own clothes is nothing compared to the reaction of other members of your household when you do the same to theirs.

• **Planning and preparation** are the keys to successful entertaining; setting yourself realistic targets comes a close third. It is far more important that everyone – yourself included – has a good, and relaxing, time than that you impress your friends with your gastronomic expertise.

• **If you aren't confident of your culinary skills**, come up with imaginative alternatives to dinner parties. Let supermarkets, caterers, restaurants or – if you are really at the end of your tether – the local takeaway do the work for you.

• **Make weekend guests feel at home** without turning yourself into a martyr. As with dinner parties, they won't be able to relax if you don't.

• **Remember that the price of good help** round the house is far above rubies. Treat anyone who works for you with courtesy and respect – and pay them on time.

BIBLIOGRAPHY

Mrs Beeton's Book of Household Management (Oxford World's Classics, 2000)

Mrs Beeton's Cookery Book (new edition, Ward Lock, 1911)

Nigel Browning & Jane Moseley, *Household Management for Men* (Cassell, 2003)

Mrs Danvers, *Red Wine on the Carpet* (Swan Hill, 2007)

Debrett's A–Z of Modern Manners (Debrett's, 2008)

Elizabeth Drury, *Victorian Household Hints* (Past Times, 1981)

Good Housekeeping, *The Best of the 1950s* (Collins & Brown, 2008)

Frances Halahan, *Household Secrets: Advice from National Trust Experts* (National Trust, 2006)

Angela Holdsworth, *Out of the Doll's House* (BBC, 1988)

The 'Isobel' Handbooks, *Things a Woman Wants to Know* (Pearson, c. 1900)

Aggie MacKenzie, *Ask Aggie* (Penguin, 2009)

John Morgan *Debrett's New Guide to Etiquette and Modern Manners* (Headline, 1996)

Nancy Mitford (ed.) *Noblesse Oblige* (Hamish Hamilton, 1956)

The National Trust, *The National Trust Manual of Housekeeping* (National Trust, 2011)

Kay Smallshaw, *How to Run Your Home Without Help* (Persephone Books, 2005)

I also gleaned useful information from the websites **www.chamois.com** and **www.marthastewart.com**, and from the wonderful and timely BBC TV series *If Walls Could Talk*.

Index